WHAT PEOPLE
ARE S

T0151588

Get ready to be challenged, inspired, and equipped! In Finding Happy, Chad Kneller helps you discover the 10 keys that will help take you where you want to go. It's an easy and motivational read and when you're finished, you'll want to pick it back up and read it again!

Michael Fletcher,
(Senior Pastor Manna Church Fayetteville, NC)
www.mannachurch.org

A page-turning, inspiring journey of a remarkable man who truly found happy and guides you on the path that can get you there as well. This is a book that will help all who read it! Chad Kneller is one of those rare people that one feels blessed to know. I believe many people will relate to the true story he shares about his life and the lessons cultivated along the way. You will experience an array of emotions as Chad shares how he went from being on the verge of giving up to a life that is changing people around the world. One thing is certain; when you finish this well written, phenomenal book, you will find happy for yourself! Truly a must-read. (5 stars)

Joshua Denne
(Entrepreneur, Investor, Marketing Strategist)
www.joshuadenne.com

This is a must-read for all and is in my top favorite books lineup. Chad is a master communicator and an authentic voice who is anointed and appointed for this hour! It was my privilege and equally a pleasure to read his story. I recommend this book to anyone who is looking for more genuine happiness in their life. The advice is sound and the principles are timeless. An all-around amazing read!

Dr. Ronnie Pierce, D.D.
(Founder, Senior Pastor Monterey Worship Center
President, Ronnie Pierce Ministries, Inc. Monterey, TN, USA)
www.ronniepierce.org

Success is different things to different people. I describe it as a steady progression toward a worthwhile goal! It's the journey, not a destination! You have taken what there was to learn from the great philosophers like Jim Rohn and applied it to your life, and he like others took most of what they taught from the Bible. I loved what you wrote about relationships and how important they are. The business opportunities come and go, but the relationships are the true equity in life. Congratulations on your book, and thank you for sharing it with me. Much continued success.

Ben Kane
(Entrepreneur, Business Owner, Franchise Consultant)

Finding Happy is a must-read! Chad provides such an inspirational story of hope that brings the reader from the reality of struggle and depression into the light of triumph and fulfillment. His story, his words, and his 10 keys are perfectly applicable during the ever-elusive pursuit of happiness. Chad lays the groundwork to help you find your own "happy". Chad Kneller is the epitome of a learner, a leader, and a man after God's own heart. He is the kind of guy that you want to follow, and Finding Happy is an excellent first step.

Eli Marshall
(Husband, Father, Entrepreneur, Lion Chaser Goal Smasher)

Chad is a game changer who helps men and women rise up to become who they were created to be. His book is a raw and unfiltered story of loss, struggle, victory, and redemption.

Tammy Kling
(CEO, The Conversation)

Thank you for sharing your book with me. I love the stories that are woven into the very fabric of the material. I think it's going to help so many and it's written very well. Hard to put down.

Cindy Pentecost
(President, It Works Gives Back Foundation)

Happiness is a choice, not a result.

Nothing will make you happy,
until you choose to be happy.

No person will make you happy,
until you decide to be happy.

Your happiness will not come to you,
it can only come from you.

Jim Rohn

FINDING HAPPY

 10 KEYS TO LIVING AN EXTRAORDINARY LIFE

CHAD KNELLER

Success is not the key to happiness.

Happiness is the key to success.

It is a wonderful thing awaiting your discovery.

Clovercroft Publishing

Finding Happy: 10 Keys to Living an Extraordinary Life

Published by Clovercroft Publishing, Franklin, Tennessee

Scripture taken from THE HOLY BIBLE, NEW INTERNATIONAL VERSION®, NIV® Copyright © 1973, 1978, 1984, 2011 by Biblica, Inc.™ Used by permission. All rights reserved worldwide.

Edited by Adept Content Solutions

Cover Design by Glendo Grider

Interior Layout Design by Adept Content Solutions

Printed in the United States of America

ISBN: 978-1-948484-30-5 (trade paperback)
ISBN: 978-1-948484-33-6 (hardcover)

CONTENTS

FOREWORD

In today's culture of unlimited self-help libraries, we rarely see stories that give a raw and transparent view into the heart of a man and his journey. *Finding Happy* isn't another manual with steps for success; it is an open and honest look through the eyes of someone whose life has been viewed from both rock bottom and on top.

These days and times we want someone to tell us the short path to success, or the immediate fix to our circumstances. It is rare to find someone who helps us look into the mirror of what it really takes to see personal change. For more than ten years my wife and I have had the privilege of walking along side the Kneller family on part of their journey to *Finding Happy*. Our lives have been impacted time and again by their pursuit of not only one another, but also their pursuit of family, faith, and excellence in business. Throughout these pages Chad brings a relatable and honest look at the heart of a man who recognizes what needs to change personally before he can impact the world around him. It is hard to find leaders who can lean forward in the trenches of success while being an open book about life's hardest self-inflicted past lessons. Having trained leaders in twelve countries over the last twenty years, I have come to love Chad's raw honesty about how he harnesses these past mistakes to build his future. Many leaders have a difficult time finding balance between faith, family, and calling. Others are enslaved by their past mistakes, which can create a life lid that keeps them bound from their true potential.

In this book, Chad gives us a glimpse of how our journey to success begins from within and the challenges that this can bring. Whether you are struggling to get by or sitting atop the corporate ladder, Chad's writings will challenge you to ask "why" you do what you do, "what and whom" you're doing it for, and most importantly "how" you can live a life full of joy and happiness. He's one of few leaders that truly enjoys his successes instead of letting them become a burden to maintain. *Finding Happy* is Chad's way of opening his heart and life experiences to help others leap forward to success and avoid his mistakes. It is a message that teaches us how we can learn to take the hand dealt to us by life of past pain and circumstance and still live a life fulfilled. Read it with an open heart and mind. Let *Finding Happy* become a personal mission for you. Let Chad's story guide you there. If you desire to see your life change and move from frustration to freedom, from hopelessness to a great future, then your life will be changed on this journey to *Finding Happy.* Thank you, Chad, for being man enough to share your journey on the road from despair to fulfillment, and more importantly for teaching us how every story that seems hopeless can turn into a legacy of happiness, success, and a fulfilling life.

Delane Hulen
CEO Acuitus International
Brother & Friend

DEDICATION

This book started off as a memoir for my wife, Jaree; my sons, Gavin and Elijah; my daughter, Ava; and the many unborn grandchildren whom I have yet to meet. I had too much to share to just keep it to myself. The information in this book comes from over a decade of study, application, and refinement. I have learned that people don't know what they don't know, and I am honored to teach others that there is hope and that life is not to only be endured but enjoyed.

As I began writing this book, I realized that I wanted to write the book that I so desperately needed in my twenties. If I had read this book at a young age, I would have begun the process of change much sooner. Meeting Jaree in 2003 drastically altered the trajectory of my life. I began to want to change, to believe that it was possible, and that I was worthy of a better life.

I also dedicate this to my siblings: Misty, Brett, and Skye. We have all had our challenges with finding happiness, and it cost my youngest brother his life in 1999. If this book can stop one person from dying prematurely, then I count it as a huge success.

ACKNOWLEDGMENTS

At the risk of missing many, I have to mention a few people who have played key roles in this book and in my life.

Dave and Marla Kneller, you are fighters and encouragers. You have always believed in me, no matter how crazy my ideas, and instilled a "you can do anything" attitude in me since birth. You taught me about marriage and commitment by your life example. I thoroughly enjoyed having you stay in my home after your retirement. It was a wonderful experience and created lifelong memories for my whole family and myself.

Josh Denne and Rick Dauenbaugh, you both believed in me when I was down but not out and taught me what "service to many" looks like.

Ken Graham, Michael Fletcher, Wayne Tate, Ron Butler, Brad Fancher, Jim Frease, Henry/Alex Seeley, Paul Bergin, and Jeremy/Rebecca Graham, you have all left tattoos on my heart.

Patricia Punches, you have been a constant source of joy and support over the years and an example of someone who loves passionately and is a bright light in this world.

Delane Hulen, John Renken, Sam Robins, Glendo Grider, and Quintin Conway, you are my five brothers from another mother who know all about me and like me anyway. You fellas are all true friends in every sense of the word. I would also like to thank Skyler Holt, Josh Denne, Wayne Tate, and the Adept Content Solutions team for going through the manuscript line by line and assisting in the editing process.

Tammy Kling, Tiarra Tompkins, and Larry Carpenter, you each made this a wonderful and enjoyable experience. I appreciate your commitment to excellence and thank you for guiding me each step of the way through telling my story in a clear and understandable way. I have worked with a number of professionals over the years, and you are all masters of your craft. Thank you for your selfless dedication, wisdom, and coaching.

INTRODUCTION

What were you born to do? This is a question every human must answer at some point in his or her life, but the answer does not come quickly. Unless you were born with a unique calling or you knew you were a musical prodigy at the age of six, it has probably been challenging to define your purpose.

In the journey to discover what you were born to do, there is a lot of struggle.

And the struggle is real.

I spent a lot of years in the pain and struggle of *Finding Happy*.

Like many people, I tried to fill myself with a lot of things that did not make me happy, or that were short-term solutions. A job, a drink, and even relationships. None of those things can make you happy, at least not for very long.

Finding Happy is a worthwhile endeavor because life is short. I've had coaches and mentors along the way and I hope you do too. I wrote this book because I want to help you. Although it life. My time in the military taught me that I am capable of doing far more than I had ever thought possible. We all are.

Two things I learned in the Army are resilience and adaptation. You had better be able to adapt to constantly changing circumstances and pressure. When the Army finds out you are scared of heights, they send you to air assault school to rappel out of helicopters or airborne school to jump out of airplanes. I learned how to live in a stressful environment 24/7 and to accept it as normal.

It's amazing what we can get used to. In basic training I was as far from happy as I ever thought I would be. Getting yelled at, being shamed, embarrassed, and constantly pushed to muscle failure is not much fun—and definitely nowhere near happiness. However, it was an escape from Illinois and a great first step in discovering who I was. I didn't realize it at the time, but I had already become quite the "escape artist." At fifteen, I discovered alcohol, and by seventeen, there was no happiness without it. Somewhere along the way, I bought into the lie that alcohol was a requirement for happiness and that I was so much more fun when intoxicated.

I imagine that you can relate to some level. We all have a past and we all have some type of pain associated with it. What I have learned is some of that pain can actually be used as fuel for our future. Most people are familiar with the term post-traumatic stress disorder (PTSD) but less are familiar with the term post-traumatic growth (PTG). For many, their past becomes debilitating to their future, but for some the mess becomes their message and they find purpose beyond their pain. My hope is that you will discover your purpose and walk out the fullness of your destiny and calling.

Basic training taught me how to focus on the here and now. I ended up graduating at the head of my class, earned my first promotion, and was ready to move on to bigger and better things. During the next three years, I would relocate several times, and live in Fort Riley, Kansas; Fulda, Germany, and Fort Stewart, Georgia. Fort Riley is a small military town, and is best known for the origin of the Spanish flu pandemic that killed 3–5 percent of the world's population. There were 50,000 soldiers stationed in the town during the start of this epidemic, and it is largely suspected that the flu originated there. The flu virus infected 500 million people around the world including people on remote Pacific islands and in the Arctic and resulted in hundreds of millions of deaths. When I arrived there, the days were filled with pain and the nights were lonely as I adjusted to my new assignment. I will never forget arriving and heading straight into the field in November without the proper winter equipment. Within a week I was second-guessing my decision to join the service. It doesn't take too many nights of guarding and digging holes at 2:00 a.m. with Kansas winds trying to knock you over to question your choices that led you there. Those years away from home were filled with many lonely nights.

With each assignment the loneliness never left.

I remember arriving in Germany on December 23, 1992, and still feeling so empty and lonely. It would be something I would battle for years. It was like there was this dark cloud hanging over my head that would never go away. During those years, I was deeply depressed. The only time I felt relief was when I went out drinking with the guys. This led to a pattern of living for the weekend and just surviving through the week. I hid it well, but I was dying inside and didn't know why.

After three years I finished my Army commitment and was ready to tackle bigger and better things. I spent the last year of my time in the Army taking personality tests and exploring career options. None of the traditional careers or employment opportunities appealed to me at all, and I just knew I wanted to do something big, something that wasn't the norm.

When I left the Army on July 30, 1994, my first idea was to become an actor. It seemed like a great idea at the time. Go big or go home, right? I was scared to death of speaking in front of people, but I was excited about all the challenges that acting school would bring.

My father was a top executive at a car manufacturing plant in Illinois and helped me get a part-time job there to supplement my income while I pursued my dream. I only worked Mondays and Fridays and could focus on school the rest of the week. I felt accomplished because I had done my time, left the Army, and learned a lot, but I was excited about the future! Like most young men at twenty-one, I was ready to take on the world.

I was once told that a rocket ship on the way to the moon is off track 97 percent of the time and has to make constant adjustments to stay on course or it will completely miss its target. Our lives are the same way. When I look back to these decisions, I see how important they all were. We have to constantly be changing and adapting to stay on course to our ultimate destination. When life gets stale, it is a sure-tell sign that we have drifted off course. The great news is that we can choose to make adjustments whenever we like. You can reinvent yourself and do a complete 180 turn if that's what gets you back on track.

There are a lot of detours on the road to happiness, and I found them all.

Maybe you took a shortcut to happiness and didn't experience what I did, or perhaps you found your own ditches to fall into. The important thing to remember is that a ditch is just a ditch. Get out, and don't stay in it. If you need a tow truck, don't panic; there's always a way out of the ditch.

My journey is funny when I look back at it, but it wasn't at the time. I traveled through a lot of different phases thinking that it was my life path. I did not know that some of those phases were just big detours and dead ends.

In 1994 I discovered this thing called karaoke. I had already become quite the partier during high school and in my time in the Army, but college was a whole new level. It introduced me to marijuana, shrooms, acid, and some other drugs of the day. In college I got a PhD in partying! Ultimately, I was asked to sing in my first band. I remember thinking, *Wow! I could totally do this for a living!*

I loved to listen to Nirvana, Pearl Jam, Soundgarden, Stone Temple Pilots, and many other rock bands back then. Some of them were my heroes. Interestingly enough, many of the artists I loved so much have either died from suicide or drug overdoses in the last few years. Not the best role models. Talk about being on the wrong path!

I remember watching *The Doors* movie and *Tombstone* over and over, thinking, *I'm going to fight like Doc Holiday and party like Jim Morrison.* For almost the next decade this would become my life mission statement. I didn't realize it at the time, but it was a very unhealthy vow. The seed had been planted, and the lyrics that played over and over in my head spoke death and destruction. Today I know better, but back then I didn't.

What thoughts are you allowing to establish and define the foundation of your life?

_____

_____

_____

_____

_____

My first real rock band was called the Mountain Oysters. When the headliner canceled at our first show, we were asked to play the whole night. This wasn't going to be easy, so I did what I had always done since age fifteen when I got nervous or overly excited—I started drinking alcohol.

> **Thoughts are powerful things.**
> **Whatever a man thinks, so he is.**

We suffered through the night playing '90s covers, but our first original, titled "Painkillers," was a huge hit. I was instantly addicted to the idea of fame, fortune, and living the rock and roll lifestyle. It was an adrenaline rush for sure! One of the things I tell parents today is to be aware of that adrenaline rush and the effect it can have on our kids whether it's a video game, the rush of the kill, the achievement, the next level, or a party. What if we could create that same rush in a healthy way? Maybe with a family hike every week or something that can build our children's lives and not destroy them.

The key is to stay proactive in our leadership goals for our families and ourselves and to recognize the things that the enemy of our soul would love to destroy us with.

Looking back, of course we all wish we could hit rewind. Some people say they would not trade their bad experiences for anything because it made them who they are, but there are certain moments of my life I'm not willing to repeat. I hope by telling my own story that I can give you some insight into yours and impact your journey to success.

If the road has been hard, have faith! You are definitely not alone, and I'm excited to be a part of your journey. You were not created just to endure life but also to enjoy life!

By 1999, I had dropped out of college twice, received about every misdemeanor you could imagine, experimented with a whole new slew of drugs, and gone full-time at the automotive plant working second shift. Other than band gigs on the weekends, I was miserable. By this point, I lived in an old weigh station with about six to seven roommates at any given time. We only had half a bathroom.

Don't laugh. It's a stark contrast from where I am today, and it was a dark, dark season of my life. I was running one hundred miles per hour in the wrong direction.

I was determined to do music for a living and nothing else. My new band was writing originals, and we went into the studio and recorded our first album. This was going to be my ticket out of the car business.

So many things seemed to be going right at this time. We were packing clubs, jamming with incredible bands, having our songs played on the radio, and even spent an hour after one show signing autographs. I remember pulling up to a stoplight while one of our songs was playing on the local radio and seeing a guy in the car next to me jamming out with the windows rolled down. I had no idea who this guy was, but he clearly loved what he was listening to—a song I had written. I just knew I would soon be touring the world, living in hotels, and partying like a rock star. It seemed like things were going so well, but when I look back now, I can clearly see that I was sowing seeds of destruction.

What dreams have you dreamt that perhaps you shouldn't have?

_____

_____

_____

_____

_____

CHAPTER 2

A WOMAN AND
MY BROTHER

Somewhere along the way, I fell for a woman who was older than me and had four kids. Not sure what I was thinking at the time, but in some very codependent and unhealthy way, we thought we needed each other. Back then I was always tuned into the "what's in it for me?" radio station (WIIFM), so this woman always took second place to my dreams and needs.

Partially due to my neglect and selfishness, "my girl" and one of my best friends got together. This seemed like the end of my life at the time. I had been completely and totally betrayed. If you can't trust your closest friends, then whom can you trust? This led into one of the most profound, depressing times of my life. At twenty-five years old, I was moving home once again.

I was suicidal during this time in my life; the next year was like a fog. I don't think I paid attention to anyone or anything around me. I was miserable, destroyed inside, and consumed with my own selfishness. Have you ever been so involved in your own personal tragedy that you can't see anyone else's?

May 1, 1999, is a day I will never forget.

One Friday night, I got a call at work that my younger brother Skye, who was fifteen at the time, had gone missing. He had taken my sister's car and disappeared. He had driven by his ex-girlfriend's house, showed her that he had a gun, and then went missing. It had been hours, and no one had seen or heard from him. We were all very worried but hoping for the best. Skye had taken my car when he was younger and had a reputation for getting into trouble. He was that kid who had no fear and lived like every day was his last.

I will never forget waking up to my father screaming that Skye had died.

Some stranger knocked on the door around 10:00 a.m. in the morning to let us know that Skye was gone. He had shot himself in the head with his friend's parent's gun. He left a note for each of us to let us know he loved us. One of the motivations for me to write this book is in memory of my brother Skye. If the words in these pages can save one life, than this is all worth it.

When I found out the news, all I could mutter was a weak, "It should have been me."

When something like this happens, everyone directly or indirectly involved feels some sort of responsibility. My little brother's girlfriend had broken up with him a few days before, and when he tried to talk to me, I just blew him off. I was wallowing in my own depression and didn't see how badly he was hurting. My parents had gone away for a short weekend and wondered if not leaving would have changed anything. Each one of us sunk deeper into the what-ifs.

Skye had asked his friend to drive in the car with him but he didn't. This type of situation causes so many what-ifs and "wish I would haves." Life is so short. Make sure you tell those that you love how you feel often. Tomorrow isn't promised to anyone, and today is a gift, which is why we call it the present. I cherish every memory that I spent with my little bro. I have many fond memories of Skye Bradley Kneller and hope to see him again one day.

From that moment on, things went from bad to worse. My drinking and drug use intensified to dangerous levels and within nine months I had reconnected with my previous girlfriend and ruined that relationship, quit my job, and left my band. I did not want to live anymore, but after seeing what my parents had gone through with my brother, I couldn't bear the thought of putting them through any more pain. I needed to get away from all of it, so I found a way.

In January of 2000, I quit my job, cashed out the $7000 that was in my 401K from my five years at the car factory, grabbed my brother Brett, and disappeared into the mountains of Ari-

> **When you don't realize that you are made for more, you only live up to the low expectations you've set for yourself.**

zona. I needed to sober up and get away from it all. We bought a book called *Hidden Arizona* and headed west. I thought that maybe hiking into the Grand Canyon or writing music at the top of Cathedral Rock in Sedona, Arizona, would give me a new perspective. I will always cherish that time with my brother Brett. We climbed mountains, explored caves, fished in lakes, hiked the Grand Canyon, explored Sedona, ate steak in Tombstone, and toured the Biosphere 2.

In March of that same year, my ex-girlfriend got in touch with me; we decided to give our relationship another shot and get married. Talk about old things you shouldn't pick up again. The old things are always going to come back to you. Giving this relationship another chance turned out to be a big mistake;

neither one of us had changed, and we had no foundation to build on. At best, we were building a house out of straw.

Our marriage had about as much chance to succeed as a fish living on top of a roof. Within six months, we were separated (and divorced shortly after). Then came more bands and more roommates, more parties, and more wasted life. I had finally bottomed out.

These were the darkest days of my life.

If you've ever been there, you can look back and see how much life you've wasted. When you don't realize that you are made for more, you only live up to the low expectations you've set for yourself. I felt trapped in a life that I didn't want to live.

CHAPTER 3

SMALL MIRACLES

On October 22, 2001, something incredible happened. By this point I was twenty-eight, flat broke, going back to college, and sleeping on my friend's floor. My sister called and asked me to meet her at a place called Shooters Lounge to have a drink. I had no desire to go, but it was her birthday so I went anyway.

To my surprise, her ex-boyfriend Ryan was also there, and he had a friend with him, a guy named Josh from California.

Josh was different.

Have you ever met someone who had a rare light about them? Someone whose eyes pierce through to your very soul? Someone who is excited and passionate about the world? It turned out that Ryan had moved to California, started a business, and came back to Illinois to meet with prospective business partners. Josh was there to meet Ryan's friends and share a new and exciting business with them!

My sister and I had not made the list, but we were at the right place at the right time. I could tell right away that there was something super special about this guy Josh. He was so full of life and *happy*. Maybe if I could just hang out with this guy, I could be happy also. He gave a short modified presentation to me about his business and scribbled some numbers on a napkin that got me really excited.

Josh told me an incredible story about how he had gotten in trouble, gone to prison, and then found a company that helped him go from making nine dollars an hour in a machine shop to making more than six figures every year. He said, "If you would come with me to Ohio, I would be willing to pay for your hotel room and help get you educated and involved in this company." He offered to take my sister and I to a training session that next weekend on his dime. The only problem was that my band had a show that same weekend.

Something inside me screamed, "I need to be at that meeting!" If you ever hear that voice, you definitely need to listen to it. I convinced my guitar player to sing at that one show and went to the event. I soon realized I had hit the jackpot with Josh. There were hundreds of people attending this training, and Josh was a featured speaker who had already found success. He gave me my first Jim Rohn CD and exposed me to an entire life that I never knew. It was the first time I began to fill my mind with positive words, thoughts, and actions that would lead to the baby steps to inspire real change. It didn't happen overnight. This guy was my first mentor and I gravitated toward him. I believed in him, and he believed in me.

He taught me to live a life of inspiration, leadership, and self-improvement. He introduced me to a world of setting goals and being accountable for them.

This one chance meeting opened my eyes to an entirely new world. I couldn't believe that Josh was not only the speaker but also the catalyst and such a successful man, and yet, he wanted to be friends with me! Over the next two years, he would teach me everything I needed to know to begin the journey to finally *Finding Happy*. He made it clear that I had to do the hard work and change my mindset at the same time.

"Chad, if you will just change, everything will change for you."

Josh reminded me that anything was possible and that my past did not have to equal my future. He was a man who sowed into my life so much at the time and still does to this day, expecting nothing in return. He was foreshadowing the type of man I would eventually become.

I remember giving a presentation at a meeting and saying, "I am well on my way to being a six figure earner."

> **If you will just change, everything will
> change for you.**

After the presentation, Josh pulled me to the side and asked what my best month had been, and I told him a little over two thousand dollars. He said, "Chad, there is no reason to exaggerate the truth and lie about your success. Just work hard, and let the results speak for themselves." I remember feeling defensive at first but later appreciating the correction. He was right about confronting me. It was my first lesson in having a true friend correct me in love. I had never experienced a friend with this type of courage before.

I am forever grateful for the seeds that Josh planted in my life and all the lessons he taught me in that season. Who is it that plants the seed of truth in your life?

_____

_____

_____

_____

_____

If you've had a mentor who made you feel defensive because
they called you out, go back and think on the advice they gave
you because it may uncover some blind spots.

CHAPTER 4

BE SURE TO GET YOUR HOPES UP

I wonder who the first person was who said: "Don't get your hopes up."

What a horrible philosophy.

I would like to ask him or her, "What should I do with my hopes? Should I flush them down the toilet with my dreams?"

If we don't have hopes and dreams, then what do we have? I have learned to guard and protect my hopes and dreams and care for them every day. You have to nurture them like a mother and defend them like a father. You should *never* lose hope. As long as you have hope, you have something to be excited about and happy for.

Some of the first original song lyrics I ever sang and played guitar to were:

An impossible dream is an untouchable dream for those too foolish to try.

A crazy sensation is a wasted temptation when pushed to the back of the mind.

We will all meet the roaring river that takes us from where we wish to roam.

The foolish man will walk away, and the wise man will look for a stepping-stone.

It's OK to dream.

Dream hard enough, and it might come true yeah.

The future isn't set in stone, we have to make it.

It's OK to dream.

Dream hard enough, and it might come true yeah.

The future isn't set in stone, we have to take it.

—Jeff Sullivan

So, we do have a part to play, and we have the freedom to make choices every day that will serve or rob us of our futures. So many of my dreams have come true that I know it's possible for yours too. My wife, Jaree, came up with a quote a few years ago that changed our world. She said, "You have got to *dream big*. You have to *dream so big* that God has to step in and move on your behalf." If you can accomplish your dreams in your own strength, then you are not dreaming big enough!

 1. Always *dreaming big* is a key to happiness!

What dreams are you dreaming right now?

_____

_____

_____

_____

_____

_____

Did you know that what you do matters? The decisions we make lead to other events and decisions. This continues until the end. We have choices to make every single day that not only affect us but also many others around us.

Are you making choices that add value to the lives of others, or are you only tuned into the "what's in it for me" (WIIFM) radio station? For me, the '90s were full of mistakes, and I didn't take responsibility for them at the time. I remember being convinced that I would die at age twenty-seven since Jim Morrison, Jimi Hendrix, and Kurt Cobain had.

Once you get that thought in your head, it takes root like a weed, grows violently, and wraps around your heart. I am very fortunate that I escaped my self-sabotaging intentions. Turns out I was only holding myself back from that which I wanted. Once I realized this and was willing to let that go, I found that I could achieve so much more.

When you live with that type of mentality, you don't even consider future consequences caused by problems created today. I have learned over the last ten years that each of us will be remembered as problem makers or problem solvers. What you do today and everyday matters. You matter!

CHAPTER 5

LOVE ASSUMES THE BEST

I once heard that love assumes the best and fear assumes the worst, and I believe it. The world is full of cynics and gossips but in desperate need of encouragers and difference makers. I remember feeling like I had wasted my life and there was no turning back. Do you have difference makers in your life? Are you aspiring to become a difference maker in the lives of others?

> **The world is full of cynics and gossips but in desperate need of encouragers and difference makers.**

The truth is that as people we can make new choices that will bring new results. You can change your current chosen trajectory. You are not a bird. You don't have to fly south every winter.

You can choose to become an entirely different person. If you are not satisfied with who you are at this moment, stop saying "one day," and let today be day óne!

Unexpectedly Finding My Wife

August 24, 2003, was another day that would radically change my life forever. I was singing with One Shot Twice and our drummer's son's best friend had died in a car wreck. We decided to partner with the family and do a benefit. There was going to be six bands, and I was going to run the sound for the day. We were at a little bar in Hudson, Illinois, called the Sitting Bull. I remember being disappointed because a girl I had been dating had to cancel at the last minute. Another disappointment in life.

I was focused on the sound and the bands when *she* walked in—a beautiful stranger. When I saw Jaree, the sight of her literally took my breath away because she was so incredibly beautiful. She didn't fit in at that little place and was completely out of my league. She was wearing the most incredible white dress and had the most infectious smile. I couldn't stop staring. All I could mutter to my friend Tim was, "She is my future wife." He elbowed me and said, "No, she's *my* future wife."

I knew I had to meet her but was nervous about the how. Maybe an hour later my band played, and Jaree was watching. My attention was on her most of the time although I didn't want her to know. After we were done, she approached me and thanked me for volunteering to play and assist with the benefit.

I asked for her phone number, and she actually gave it to me! I could not believe it! Later that night, I called Jaree and asked her if she wanted to meet me for karaoke. She met me with one of her friends, and I sang, we danced, we kissed, and she came home with me.

That was fourteen years ago, and we have been inseparable since. Jaree had traveled two hours to attend the benefit because the guy who passed was a very close friend. How ironic that such a tragic event would lead me to finding my forever bride. If this tragic event hadn't happened, I may have never met my wife. If I had never met Jaree, then we would have never had our three kiddos. Sometimes one person's tragedy can lead to another person's new beginning. That was the case for Jaree and me.

When I look back on that day, I can honestly say that it was the last thing I expected. After years of searching, partying, girlfriends, frenemies, and betrayal, finding my forever bride wasn't even a possibility in my mind. Meeting Jaree changed my life forever and lit a fire that I didn't even know was in me. I thought maybe I had already missed my opportunity. For some reason, I was given a second chance.

Why was I given a second chance in life? I don't know. I'm not sure I'm supposed to know.

Maybe it was because when I hit rock bottom, I sent up a desperation prayer. I said, "God, I need your help. Trying to do this all on my own just isn't working." I didn't feel anything or hear a response at the time, but looking back, I now believe that saying that prayer was crucial. I believe that God heard me and sent me the woman who would give me the courage to change.

Jaree would tell you that meeting me saved her life too. When she arrived at that benefit she was looking for a way to escape from her abusive boyfriend. She had already been wounded, broken, and fractured by too many other men, but this guy was the worst. He had wooed her by treating her like a princess and then he would tear her down. Day by day and piece by piece, he had made her totally reliant on him. She had also recently prayed, and I was part of the answer that she needed. Together we would fill each other's gaps and call out the greatness in each other.

We had a lot of work to do that can be summed up by the first time I met Jaree's father.

Jaree said, "Dad, I want you to meet my new boyfriend," and he said, "Does this one at least have a driver's license?" He was semi-joking, and I nervously laughed it off, but the truth was that I had in fact lost my driver's license. It had been suspended. Fortunately, I was in the process of getting it back and did within weeks of that meeting. It was years later before Alan discovered that I didn't have a license when we met. We laugh about it now, but it wasn't very funny at the time.

CHAPTER 6

⤬

LIFE IS CONNECTED

What if you knew from the beginning of your life that everything is connected? What if you knew that you'd look back and be transformed?

You have probably heard that for every cause there is an effect. If you were faced with four doors, choosing one would mean you are not choosing the other three. Behind every door is another set of doors. Most doors represent small choices, but, occasionally, we open the door that leads us to a life-changing connection. Over the years, I have met several people whose names begin with the letter "J" who have changed my life. The first two were Josh and Jaree. About two weeks into my new relationship with Jaree, Josh was in town, and we all went out to do karaoke. That was the thing to do at the time. You can imagine my surprise and embarrassment when I was taken away for having six warrants out for my arrest.

One was for public urination, as embarrassing as that was, and the others were almost as bad. Without hesitation, Josh and Jaree went to the ATM and got the money to bail me out of jail. That's when I knew I had found the right woman and the right friend. If they would walk with me through my past mistakes, then I knew we could all build a future together. *True friends are those people who know everything about you and love you anyway.*

At the time I met Jaree, I was earning $2000 in a good month, and she had started waitressing at Cracker Barrel. My arrest was maybe two weeks into our relationship. What had started off being a few hundred dollars in tickets would end up costing us thousands of dollars and a two-week stay in jail. Going to jail was a wake-up call for me and was not helpful to our financial situation. I was reminded of the board game Monopoly: do not pass go and do not collect $200. Only this was my life, not a game.

Jail was a culmination of all the bad decisions that I had made over the last decade. Time exposed every area of my life during this season, and I got to sit in the Big House for two weeks and reflect and reset. I see now how perfect the timing was in all this. Without jail, I'm not sure I would have ever slowed down enough to focus on my life and what needed to change. Sometimes we have to slow down to speed up. At least that is what jail did for me.

During those two weeks in my cell, I picked up a Bible and read the entire book for the very first time. I had heard some of the stories, but this time the book came to life. I had already changed much of my thinking, but this time I felt a change happening to my heart. I knew that when I left jail, I would implement major life changes, and my life was going to be completely different. This song called "The Reason" by a band called Hoobastank kept playing over and over while I was in jail, and I will never forget the lyrics.

I've found a reason for me.

To change who I used to be.

A reason to start over new.

And the reason is you.

Humble Beginnings

I've always heard that behind every man is an amazing *woman*. This is 100 percent true in my case. The day Jaree came into my life, my world was rocked, and it still is to this day. My bride has consistently stretched and challenged me in every way. God knew it was going to take an extremely strong-willed woman to change me, and that is exactly who he sent. She didn't put up with any crap at all. She has always loved me fiercely, stood firm in her convictions, and not compromised on her beliefs.

We needed each other to grow, but I needed her more. I have always felt like I married up and that my greatest accomplishment in life was getting Jaree to marry me. I'm dedicated to proving to her for the rest of my life that she made the right decision.

When we got married, she was already eight months pregnant. We lived in a spare section of her grandparent's house and were living on around $500 a week. I bought her a cubic zirconia ring that cost less then one hundred and fifty dollars and my ring was even less. It was a cheap wedding in her parents sunroom with her uncle Roger officiating. "You've got about a 50/50 chance of making it," he said to us.

This statistic blew my mind. He went on to share that prearranged marriages have a better chance of succeeding. I couldn't believe it. Roger shared that most Americans lack the commitment to follow through. I see so many good people end their marriage in the name of irreconcilable differences. Truth is that we all have differences, and most of them are not irreconcilable. Irreconcilable differences generally mean that there is no hope that the couple will be able to work out their problems and save the marriage. It can also be referred to as an irretrievable breakdown of the marriage. My friend Lonnie Berger explains it as "two ticks and no dog."

Two people who are trying to suck the life out of each other. It's when both parties want to take or receive and no one is giving. This combination never works. I decided to choose right then that we would not be a divorce statistic.

Over the years, Jaree and I have had huge fights, and it was so bad at times that both of us wanted to give up. Once Jaree even went to the courthouse to file for a divorce and came back with the paperwork. I tore up those papers and said, "You are not going to get rid of me that easy!"

Back then I was always fighting against my wife instead of fighting for her. Men, now is the time to stop and think about this. Are you fighting for or against your wife?

If there's anything couples should get from this book, it's that life can be bad—awful, even—but it can get better, and there is always hope. Jaree and I were in a heated argument one day in a church parking lot before a counseling session when I said to her, "Let's go in there and tell him how psycho you really are." Surprisingly, she leaned over and whacked me in the face with her fist! It's ironic now, looking back, that we had a fight in the church parking lot.

Perhaps she punched me only to prove my point. Regardless, I pulled over and got out of the car. I was furious! I was bleeding and yelling, and she was apologizing and begging me to get back in the car. That fight only got worse from there, but suffice it to say we always had huge fights from early on, and it was only by God's grace that we have made it through. Love was not enough. We had to learn that marriage is much more about giving than receiving and to stop being two ticks with no dog. Here is an excerpt from my friend Lonnie Berger's study titled "Every Man a Warrior."

Not many twenty-year-old men are kind, sensitive, gentle, reliable, and not primarily focused on themselves. But a sixty-year-old man who has walked with God, loved his wife, and raised his children, develops the gentleness, understanding, insight, and wisdom that comes about as he gives up his life by focusing on his wife and children rather than himself.

When a man sees his wife's differences as a blessing, not as a threat to his manhood or a challenge to his leadership, he has grown. As men, we need to see our wives as the other side of a coin, with a perspective and set of gifts that, when brought together with our own, brings greater potential for what we can accomplish in life.

When a man sees his wife's perspective as wrong or invalid because it is different from his own and he refuses to consider its merit, he's an idiot. He is refusing to consider the advice of a person who has been specifically designed by the God of the universe to fill his gaps and cover his blind spots. What a mistake!

This does not mean that your wife's opinion is the right one and yours is wrong. She may be just as out of balance as you are. But when we listen and consider those parts of her perspective that give balance to our own, we make better decisions and fewer mistakes.

This truth was such a huge revelation to me. These words rock me every time I read them!

Here is a word of advice for my female readers: You have to make sure that your husband is getting more attention from you than his co-workers or secretary. Never let any other woman give your man more attention than you do. He wants and needs to know that he is your hero! Chances are he may not be, especially if he's betrayed your trust, or if he's lazy, or just not the leader of your household yet. Treat him like the hero anyway. Don't just see him as the man he is; see him as the man he can become. Treat him like the man God wants him to be while you're working out your issues together. Always remember that love is a choice.

In the beginning, Jaree and I didn't take personal responsibility for our issues. We took credit for what went well and blamed the other for what didn't. We both wanted a successful family, but neither one of us knew that we had major issues to clear up. Our ideas of "normal" were so different from the other. All we knew was that we needed leadership and guidance on how to be parents. We began to seek mentors out of desperation.

Just two months into our relationship, we got some incredible, yet shocking, news. We were going to be parents! Neither of us saw that coming. I'm not sure why we didn't, but I guess that goes to show how intentional we were at the time.

This news disrupted our whole world. What were we going to do? We weren't qualified to be parents. I knew that we needed help. We both wanted to bring our new baby into a safe, healthy environment, but we didn't have a clue what that looked like. I thought that I needed to get some help for Jaree, and she was thinking the same about me.

We agreed that there should be some good people out there somewhere to help us prepare. In our brainstorming, we thought about churches. Surely we could learn how to be great parents by someone at a church. However, our discussions on what type of church led to months of arguing and indecision.

One day while Jaree was working at Cracker Barrel, a pastor named Ken Graham walked into our lives. Jaree was a server at Cracker Barrel, and Ken just happened to sit at her table. I was working with a company at the time that just released a CD designed to recruit pastors. Jaree got his information for me, so I could recruit him into my business. He met with us, listened politely, and then invited us to attend church the next Friday for couples night. We visited and had a great time.

Over the next two years, Ken and his wife, Nancy, selfless-ly loved us and modeled true Christianity. They always met us where we were and never once judged us. They also didn't just talk the talk but also walked the walk. After reading the entire Bible in jail (about eighty-five pages a day), I had pages of questions for Ken!

One by one, Ken went through the list of questions with me, helping me to discover new truths. I have since become a student of the Bible. Isn't it interesting how we get instruction manuals for our car, computer, phone, and dishwasher, but no instruction on being a good parent, friend, manager of finances, business owner, or spouse? I discovered during my time in jail that all the answers to the important things in life are in the Bible.

Every year I go through the "Every Man a Warrior" (EMAW) course with a group of guys and we explore biblical principles on walking with God, marriage, children, money, sex, work, hard times, and making your life count. Every year, my life, and those of many other men, are changed because of this study. Before I discovered the Bible and EMAW, I was just winging it in all these areas. If you are a man and you want to grow, then you need to get into one of these groups! You can go to www.everymanawarrior.com today to get connected with a group near you.

After marriage, facing my past, and having child #1 on the way, I was truly excited about the future. Jaree and I had decided to become Christians and make the life-changing decision to accept Jesus Christ as our personal Lord and Savior. I was thirty years old and felt like life was finally beginning. I had heard all the stories growing up but had never taken the time to understand the magnitude of what Jesus did on earth and what he did specifically for me. I am eternally grateful for who he is and what he did. I'm not where I want to be, but I am farther than I used to be. He is the Lord of my life, and I do my best to give every area of my life to Him.

I've learned that whatever I give to God ends up blessed, and whatever I try to do on my own ends up a mess. I now understand that there is purpose beyond pain and that the best years of life are ahead and not behind. My past does not have to equal my future, and yours doesn't either. Today, the words that Josh first shared with me all those years ago have come true. "If I would change, then everything would change for me."

My friend Josh is a constant reminder in my life of what is possible. He had spent years in prison and became successful anyway. God will send you who you need at just the right time if you're patient. Wait out the pain.

Not only had Josh become financially successful but also he had completely changed. He had gone through massive personal development, and he continually encouraged me that I could be anyone and do anything. Josh was and still is one of the most incredible guys I know and biggest influences in my life. At one point in 2007 we traveled to Brazil together on a missions trip, and I remember sitting in the back of a truck somewhere in

Whatever I give to God ends up blessed, and whatever I try to do on my own ends up a mess.

Guyana describing to him how it felt to be a father and that he was going to love it someday.

Today, he has three beautiful daughters, a handsome son, and a beautiful wife, and he would tell you they are his most significant accomplishments. I was honored to be asked to read his book *Inevitable* while he wrote it and be quoted in the "What People Are Saying" section. His book was a huge inspiration for me to write *Finding Happy*.

When Josh introduced me to this world of personal development, the first person I heard about was Jim Rohn. Jim Rohn is one of the founding fathers of personal development. He was a key influencer in people's lives, like John Maxwell and Tony Robbins. Jim had these little sayings that have taken deep root in my life.

My favorite Jim Rohn coffee mug says, "Don't wish it was easier. Wish you were better."

Jim says not to not ask for fewer problems, but ask for more solutions. He said that successful people do what unsuccessful people are not willing to do. Successful people live outside of their comfort zone. Leaders are learners. Jim taught me a life philosophy that I share every time I can, which is *"if you will change then everything will change for you."* This is so true. Sometimes you've got to make radical changes.

I wish I could tell you that the day Jaree and I became Christians everything just became unicorns and rainbows, but I would be lying. Part of growing and changing is healing and unlearning. Jaree and I both had been deeply wounded in our childhoods, and we learned that hurt people hurt people. We spent a lot of time fighting against each other instead of fighting for each other. At the time I wanted to have my cake and eat it too. I wanted to be a great husband and father, but I also wanted to be that wild and crazy weekend rock star for the band I was in. Before I met Jaree, this band was my life. The other three guys in One Shot Twice were like brothers to me, and I didn't want to let them down by quitting on them. At the same time, I knew I was going to have to give up the good if I wanted to live the better life.

In November 2003, I slipped a personal letter of resignation into each of their cars during one of our gigs. It was one of our best shows, and it was a bittersweet ending to a transformational season of my life. They were witnessing my transformation as it happened, and they knew it was just a matter of time. The letters basically said, "I love you guys, you are all legends, and I am going to miss you."

New Life Requires New Mentors

Every step of the way, Jaree and I have had mentors and sought out mentors. It's my belief that everyone should be learning from someone and then paying forward the wisdom to someone else. There's learning, modeling, and teaching. All of these levels of knowledge will impact a life. When you get to the teaching stage, you're impacting a lot of lives and the process of multiplication is profound. I've participated in many growth groups and have witnessed that anyone can do anything if they really want to change, if they really take the steps to do it. I don't believe that any great information is just for us. This is why I teach others to teach others. Learning something just isn't enough.

We need to learn it and then teach someone else to teach it. I take copious notes at every class, seminar, webinar, or church as if I were going to teach the information the next day. I do my best to share everything that is impactful to me. This is how great ideas can duplicate from child to child, person to person, and nation to nation.

*Success comes from knowing that you did your best
to become the best that you are capable of becoming.*

John Wooden

CHAPTER 7

PREPARATION

Maybe the differences and conflict in your life are meant to be there? Have you ever pondered that? What if the struggle is necessary for the breakthrough? If you don't have the proper training, then the weight of an early promotion could crush you. I've discovered that God often puts two different people together to prepare you for something you cannot prepare for yourself, and it's usually for a larger purpose.

In August of 2004, less than two months into our marriage, Gavin was born. I will never forget how amazing it was to witness him being born. It was the first miracle I had ever witnessed with my own eyes. From the moment I saw him, I knew I would love him forever, take care of him, and learn how to be a great dad. Those first few months with Gavin were bittersweet. He was colicky, so Jaree didn't get much sleep. I remember the excitement of seeing him do new things every day. This whole "dad world" was incredible. I would watch Gavin for hours and enjoy every minute. I knew that I had to make changes to better provide for Gavin and Jaree but didn't know what to do next.

Shortly after Gavin was born, I was walking down the road and saw a soldier wearing the new army uniform and had the thought of going back into the service. First I went to the Air Force and then the Marines recruiter, but they weren't accepting prior service, so I went into the Army office to look into going into the Reserves or National Guard.

The recruiter there shared all the benefits with Jaree about being an Army spouse, and we both got really excited. I decided to join as a parachute rigger for two main reasons: First, I wouldn't have to deploy every year. Second, because I would be guaranteed to jump out of airplanes. I had grown out of my desire to be a rock star but was still always looking for the next thrill. Being trained to jump out of airplanes seemed like a step in the right direction.

I would be going back through some of the training at thirty that I went through at eighteen. This was exciting and humbling at the same time. I had really enjoyed the military during my first enlistment, and now I was going back into service after an eleven-year break with much more wisdom and life experience. I was going to be starting off with less rank but more pay from where I had left off in 1994. March 5, 2005, I officially entered back into active military duty.

For the next five months I would be gone training in three different states. After Fort Knox, Fort Benning, and Fort Lee we would be relocating to Fort Bragg, North Carolina, home of the 82nd Airborne!

There is something about relocating to another state that has always been so exciting for me. I've always loved moving into a new house, having new neighbors, and making new friends. What this process has taught me is that no matter where we go, we always bring ourselves with us.

"Wherever you go, there you are" (Confucius).

I have heard this phrase before but have never been ready to embrace the concept until recently. No matter where I am, who I'm with, or where I'm working, I am responsible for my happiness. No person, place, or thing can nor should be responsible for my happiness. If I allow someone else to be responsible for my happiness, I give them power over me. When I am responsible for my happiness, then I have the power.

So, what is the meaning of "Wherever you go, there you are"? It means that it does not matter if you change jobs, cities, relationships, or the style of underwear you wear, if you have not made peace and happiness within yourself, then it does not matter. Even if you find the perfect business in your ideal city after marrying your dream-come-true soul mate, you will still be you, and if you are not happy inside, then you will find fault with your outer life. You will find yourself in relationship number twenty-seven, career change fifteen, and moving every two years.

> ## Wherever you go, there you are.
> ### *Confucius*

Most people cannot recognize for themselves what happiness really is, so it becomes circumstantial. It's a marriage, a woman, a job or income that fulfills their happiness. When any one of those shifts, the happiness disappears.

Understanding true happiness is important.

We think we will relax when we "get there," when we "arrive." Then and only then will we finally be happy. We think then we can do fun things, think happy thoughts, and live a happy life. Now isn't a good time for it because we don't have this, that, or the other thing. We all must learn to be thankful for what we already have while we pursue all that we want.

The problem with starting over is that our baggage comes with us.

Whatever change we make or wherever we go doesn't matter because we can't outrun ourselves. Eventually, we have to address the real problem.

That problem is *you* and *I*.

Let's give a different perspective a try: Wherever you go, there you are. So take a deep breath and let yourself feel some peace. What are you thankful for right now in this moment?

_____

_____

_____

_____

_____

Even though Jaree and I had established a solid foundation, we still had a lot of work to do. After the Army training, we made the move to Fayetteville, North Carolina, in late 2005. The Army took great care of us, and we were able to go straight into some of the nicest new housing the military had to offer. This was an amazing upgrade from living at Jaree's grandparents' house.

Our family just didn't seem to be complete, so we added two dogs: Daisy and Capone. I settled into my new career and at age thirty-two was quickly in the best shape of my life. I was excited to serve and this time attacked each day with new vigor and purpose. As soon as we got settled, we started searching for a home church, and the first few months were extremely frustrating.

The first few churches we visited were not what we were looking for. I remember being ushered to the front row in one and being extremely uncomfortable. Jaree wanted to sprint out of the building. The first day we walked into Manna Church in Fayetteville, North Carolina, we knew we had found something special. Everyone was super friendly, and the woman who showed us around said, "If you like to be challenged and get involved, then you will love it here."

Over the next four years, Jaree and I grew so much at that church that we didn't even recognize who we used to be when we first arrived. We met many of our closest friends during those precious years. This was a season of blooming where we were planted. One of the first things we did after joining Manna Church was start a small group for young married and engaged couples. Each week we would have five to six couples at our house. Most were married, but one couple was engaged. While attending the Krueger wedding, I realized the pastor performing the ceremony was the father of a guy in our group. At the reception he began talking to me about this "Destiny and Calling" class that he was offering. Steve said they were offering the first course for free through Grace College of Divinity.

I was intrigued by the name, so I decided to sign up for it. The course was amazing. I began to discover more about my personal calling and destiny.

On one particular day, Dr. Crowther was extra excited during class and began to share an opportunity that was unfolding in Brazil. Hundreds of villages of American Indians desired to learn about Jesus. Steve was looking for people to come with him to Brazil. I just knew that I was supposed to go. Has this ever happened to you? Where you just knew you had to do something? I never had the thought to go on a missions trip, but now I had the burden to go. I asked what I needed to do to go, and Steve said just volunteer. I volunteered and ended up going to Brazil three different times watching the vision unfold.

Each choice led to the next choice, ultimately leading to Brazil. As I write this I am in a hotel room returning from Fayetteville, North Carolina, over a decade later after first meeting Steve. Today I am part of the Grace College of Divinity Advisory Board, and it all started because I joined a band, met Jaree, joined the army, went to Fort Bragg, started a small group, went to the wedding, said yes to the class, went to Brazil, and continued to be open to being used by God. All of this was in preparation for amazing things to come.

Are you willing to go and be open to new and exciting life change? The steps you take today will impact your tomorrow. Envision yourself a decade from now. You can create a new future.

CHAPTER 8

—⁂—

PAY IT FORWARD

When you are in the Army and a decision is made that you are ready to become a leader, you become recommended for the promotion board. This board is not for the faint of heart. The preparation alone requires many hours of training. The board is designed to stress you out, frustrate you, and break you. A promotion board normally has four to five senior non-commission officers.

If you have solid leaders, then they will take the time to prepare you by using mock boards. These are less stressful but still give you a taste of how the real one will feel.

Most of these promotion boards ask you questions shotgun style. This means while you are answering one question you are already being asked another from another person. So you have multiple people speaking at the same time. There are many things you can do wrong to justify immediate termination from the board. I've known people who were removed from the board in their first five minutes left waiting months for another chance.

Your senior leaders are evaluating how you perform under the most stressful situation. When you pass this board, you are given the promotable status. This means you are now qualified to go to Warrior Leadership Course (WLC), one of the final requirements to becoming a non-commissioned officer.

I will never forget attending this course in 2007. I had some fantastic instructors, but one stood out above all the rest. Sergeant First Class (SFC) Smith was extremely knowledgeable, and everyone had massive respect and admiration for this man. One day, he told me that I had five minutes to teach the rest of the class on the values of the army. I immediately went in front of the class and gave the best presentation that I could. I received amazing feedback that gave me more confidence in my abilities.

After class, he pulled me to the side and asked if he could call me "Colonel Kneller." He went on to say that my presentation was just as good as any other officer he had ever heard.

He then asked me a question, one that seared deeply into my mind, "Have you ever considered being an officer?" Up to that point, I had ruled myself out. I didn't think I had it in me. I would have to finish my bachelor's degree, request waivers because of my past, get selected, get referrals, pass another board, and go through many more months of schooling. There were too many parts to becoming an officer with a high rate of failure.

SFC Smith believed in me long before I believed in myself. His belief gave me hope, and the seed he planted grew. I have since paid it forward and encouraged other men and women in many ways. I have been able to call out the gifts in others and highlight their talents. One of my favorite definitions of leadership is "getting someone to do something they would not have done if you would not have been there." If it were not for SFC Smith being there and planting that seed, then I may have never grown beyond my comfort zone. Greatness is always found outside our comfort zone. Who has planted seeds in your life, and whose lives are you sowing into?

_____

_____

_____

_____

_____

 2. Believing in others and paying it forward is a key to happiness!

You cannot always prepare for success or failure, but just know that there may be success hiding in the failure.

Failure is the Fertilizer of Success

Denis Waitley

CHAPTER 9

PAIN RELEASES SELFISHNESS

Think about when you stub your toe, the first thing you say isn't, "I want to donate money to Africa." Sometimes we say or do things that we later regret. Why? Because we are in pain, and the only thoughts we have are about ourselves. When we are all wrapped up in ourselves, we make a very small package. Pain releases our selfishness.

> **We are wired by our creator to be givers.**
> **When we are giving, we are happy.**

So, what really makes us happy? It makes us happy to think about and serve other people. We are wired by our creator to be givers. When we are giving, we are happy. There is coming a time when all we will have left is what we have given to God. Let me share a story that will make this point.

I call it "Chicken and Diapers."

One of the days I was working, I received a call from Jaree around 4:30 p.m. asking if I would grab diapers and pick up some chicken and fries. We had a favorite little place down the road from our house that made the best chicken. So I was excited to get going and get home. As I walked out of the office, I heard my commander say, "Kneller, come here for a second." The second turned into minutes, and minutes turned into almost an hour. By now I was *hangry*, and I knew Jaree was expecting me home any second. To make things worse, it had just started raining, and I had a 4–5 minute walk to my car. As soon as I walked outside, my phone started ringing. I knew it was the "How far away are you?" call.

When you are wearing an Army uniform, you can't walk and talk at the same time, so I couldn't answer the phone until I got to my car. By the time I answered, Jaree had probably called me a dozen times, and I could hear the frustration when she asked: "Where are you?" Neither of us was happy with my answer. Being kept late at work, being in a wet uniform, and being hungry was not a good combination. That phone conversation did not end well. Imagine my mental state as I pulled into Walgreens to buy diapers. As I got out of my car, I saw a tall, slender gentleman standing by the entrance. I also noticed an old-looking truck with the hood up and a woman and small dog inside of it, avoiding the rain.

I had a feeling that this guy was going to ask me for something, and he did. He was having radiator problems. "I found a guy who can come and replace it, but I am $160 short on funds. Any chance you can help me out?" I told him that I would give him some money after I got the diapers. After checking out, I saw the man again waiting patiently outside. I had completely forgotten about him, as my mind was totally focused on chicken. I told him I would grab some money from my car, and as

I searched, I had less than a dollar in change. I wanted to give him more than that, so I decided to go back into the store and buy a pack of gum and get $20 back to help this guy out. In the store, I realized for the first time that this Walgreens had an in-store ATM. I thought, *Awesome I can give him a little more.* As I clicked through the screens, I remember thinking ,*I will get $80 to pay for half.* Next, I heard a voice that flooded my mind that said, "When you ask for something from me, do you want me to give you half?" I said, "No, sir," and got the entire $160 out of the machine. When I handed the money to this guy, he was so thankful. He immediately ran to his truck to show his wife.

I walked to my car, and after I had started the vehicle, the woman ran over and reached in through the window and gave me the biggest hug. As I drove away, one of the most incredible things happened. I looked into my rearview mirror and what I saw changed my life. The man had one arm around his wife, and the other arm had the money raised into the air. The wife had one arm around her husband, and the other was holding the dog. They were jumping up and down, spinning in circles and dancing in the rain. Unexplainable joy flooded into my heart at that moment that was worth far more than the $160 I had given away.

That was the day that I learned it is far better to give than to receive. Hebrews 13:2 says, "Do not forget to show hospitality to strangers, for by so doing some people have shown hospitality to angels without knowing it." I often wonder if those were a couple of angels and if that was a test. Just maybe the couple weren't celebrating the $160 but celebrating my passing of the test. Either way, that experience changed me forever.

To not leave you hanging, I did get the chicken, and the fries were soggy. Needless to say, Jaree wasn't happy when I walked through the door. After I shared the story with her, she was immediately thankful and excited. The only thing I remember her saying was, "You should have given them more money." Jaree has always been a huge giver, but it took a while for me to come around.

 ## 3. It is far better to give than to receive and a key to happiness.

Who are you investing your time, talent, and treasure into?

_____

_____

_____

_____

_____

Through my own struggles, I realized that I had a choice to make. I could either be the victim or I could use my pain as fuel. At some point, everyone has to ask, "Is there a purpose beyond my pain?" If there isn't a purpose, then what is life truly all about? I think it takes a higher level of maturity in a person to begin to recognize that there's a purpose to their pain instead of getting stuck in it. Have you gotten stuck in your pain? I know I have. It's no different than ending up with your car in a ditch and just walking away. Everyone has a choice to make.

If you end up in the ditch, which we all do at one point or another, you have to man up and figure out a way to get the car out of the ditch. Whether you call a tow truck or a friend to help you, it doesn't matter. Either way, it's going to be costly to get the car out of the ditch. Herein lies the point. Pain is costly. But if you are wise, there's a purpose to your pain. In the Bible, Jesus says, "Remember that if the world hates you, they hated me first" (John 15:18).

It doesn't matter if you created your pain or someone else caused it. Unfortunately, if you created it, there's a lot of shame and guilt that comes along with it. If someone else created it, it's easier to feel like the victim. Either way, there's no honor in hanging onto your pain or identifying with the victim mentality. Give your pain focus, give it purpose, and allow it to turn into success.

Author Nick Vujicic has no arms and no legs. At one point in his life, he tried to commit suicide, by drowning himself in a bathtub. It was at this point, God give him a vision of his parents alone and suffering at the thought of his death. This thought of not hurting his parents, prevented him from trying to commit suicide again. Today he's a multimillion-dollar author and speaker who travels the globe and saves souls wherever he goes. He still has no arms and no legs.

| **Give your pain purpose.** |

Has his pain changed any? I'm sure it has. What he once identified as hopelessness is now fuel to encourage and inspire hope in others. When he speaks, there are literally hundreds of thousands of people in the audience.

Can you even imagine?

I don't know what kind of job you have, but if you're a speaker, an executive, or even a rock star, you've probably been in front of thousands, but not many people have been able to speak in front of hundreds of thousands. Nick has used his pain to change lives; he has used his pain for a purpose.

Is there a purpose to your pain? Please do not backslide into thinking, "Well, you can't possibly know what my pain is about," "I experienced abuse in a relationship," "I caused a divorce," "I cheated on my wife," or, "my parents beat me." It doesn't matter what your pain was or currently is; there is a purpose in it. *Find it!* Do not let your pain weigh you down! I have broken through so many chains, and I know you can too!

Remember, pain is pain. Give your pain purpose, and make today the day that you do it.

CHAPTER 10

SHE'S A LITTLE BIT COUNTRY AND I'M A LITTLE BIT ROCK AND ROLL

4. Relationships are the key to everything in life and instrumental in *Finding Happy*.

You can't have solid relationships with others if you're still broken yourself. Eventually, you've got to let go and let God. As strange as that may sound, it's sure true. Let go of anything that's holding you back in bondage, and let God do the work in your heart.

How about your past relationships? We have all suffered through difficult relationships and have been forced to face our own weaknesses in the mirror. There will always be things to work on to become a better human being. Sometimes, in relationships the differences can feel intense and torturous. They say opposites attract; however, with opposites there is often a great deal of conflict.

Donnie and Marie Osmond used to sing a song about Marie being a little bit country and Donnie being a little bit rock and roll. My mother says that I started singing as soon as I started talking. Apparently I loved the Donnie and Marie Osmond show. I've been told that when I was two, I would run around singing using a plastic nail from my tool kit play set for a microphone.

In the 1980s, I memorized every word from the Bon Jovi *Slippery When Wet* album. I remember jumping on my bed singing all the words to the entire album for hours at a time. In my twenties, I would attend other concerts when I didn't have a show. I enjoyed evaluating and studying the front man to see if I could borrow some of his or her characteristics to better develop my own stage presence.

This one particular weekend will always stick out in my mind. My high school friend Brent loved music just as much as I did, and one weekend he said, "Hey, man, do you want to come to a couple of concerts with me?" I agreed. On one side of town, we went to a Death Metal concert, and on the other side of town, we went to a Jam For The Lamb concert. They were two completely different audiences and vibes. That night we ended up going back to the Death Metal concert, but I have never forgotten how my first experience at the Jam For The Lamb felt. The two concerts were as different as light and dark. Looking back, the darkness, which I had become so accustomed to living in, desperately fought to suffocate the light growing inside.

I had taken on the identity of a wild, psychotic, carefree person for so long that I was completely unsure if it would be possible for me to change. There is an enemy who wants to rob, steal, and kill you. He roams about the earth seeking out those he can devour. I listened to him for many years. The good news is that you can learn to tune that voice out and tune into the one who wants to give you peace, happiness, and joy. The experience at the Christian concert planted a mustard seed of faith in my heart that would grow over time. "Truly, I tell you, if you have faith as small as a mustard seed, you can say to this mountain 'Move from here to there,' and it will move. Nothing will be impossible for you" (Matt. 17:20).

When I met Jaree we would have radio wars in the car. She would always want to play country, and I would always want to play rock and roll. She would say things like, "You would sound so good singing country." I would laugh and say things like, "I wouldn't be caught dead singing that crap." In my stubbornness, I would refuse to even consider the idea.

Rock and roll had been such a huge part of my identity for so long. I was stubborn; I remember feeling that if I were to sing something else, I would be losing a huge part of my identity. The first time I sang worship music on stage at church I thought for sure the ceiling would cave in, I would be struck by lightning, and then burst into flames. To my surprise, nothing like that happened. I figured that I had already done so much wrong in my life that it was too late for me. I was so wrong. Romans 6:23 says, "For the wages of sin is death, but the gift of God is eternal life in Christ Jesus our Lord." All I had to do was ask for forgiveness, accept this free gift, change my ways, and accept Jesus as my personal Lord and Savior.

All these years later, I find myself singing mostly Christian music and even an occasional country song. It's amazing how much things can change when we decide to change. "If you will just change, everything will change for you." Growing should be a constant pursuit. After all, if we are not learning something new or contributing to someone's well-being, we are not doing what God intended.

What seeds are you planting in your spouse? How about your children? Make sure you are planting strong oaks that bring life and not dangerous weeds that bring death. Is it time for a change? Maybe it's time to completely rewrite the life you're living even down to the music you're listening to! We get so set in our old established ways and what we think we like that we refuse to listen to reason or do anything else.

What seeds have been planted within you unknowingly? Have you ever paused and asked yourself that question?

Romans 12:2 (NIV)

Do not conform to the pattern of this world, but be transformed by the renewing of your mind. Then you will be able to test and approve what God's will is— his good, pleasing and perfect will.

CHAPTER 11

GET DISCIPLINED

You can know something but not know how to execute or walk it out. One of the things I love doing is helping people bridge the gap between their dreams and their reality. Jaree and I love to assist people with fixing their dreamer muscles. In my experience, I have found the majority of people have lost the ability to use their dreamer muscles. They wind up living life in an apathetic, near-comatose state. I coach people on how to design their lives by discovering what they really want and then assist them in creating a plan to achieve it. The key is to help people understand that a dream without a plan is just a wish.

The world is full of joiners who have good intentions but no follow-through. Success takes commitment, resolve, and grit. Commitment is doing what you said you would do long after the feeling you said it in has left you. Resolve means that you will keep going and that there is no quit date. You have the resolve to complete what you started off to do.

Success also means different things to different people. For you, it may be more money, more family time, or an extra vacation every year. For others it may mean giving more to their favorite charity or organization. What about earning enough to make sure your parents are well taken care of or that you can help a child with college? For me, success is about producing great things and mentoring others to create peace in their lives. I find great fulfillment in doing things that matter with people who care and sometimes showing up in others testimonials. One of the best feelings in the world is impacting another person's life so dramatically that he or she refers to meeting you as a turning point in his or her life.

Sometimes in life, it's almost like you need a do-over. A complete life rehab!

I am a firm believer of the ability to reinvent ourselves anytime we choose. When you screw it all up, go to bed with the confidence that new grace and opportunity will be waiting the next day. We have the power to decide that, "the next three years will be much better than the last three years." We can tear up the old script and the old goals and make new ones. We can go from being ridiculously unhealthy, to being fit, fueled, and focused in a matter of months. I have heard that heart attack survivors often become the healthiest people in the world. Why is this? Maybe they finally realize that they have to change or they could die. What a huge motivator!

I remember hearing the story about Jesus' disciples and how radically they all changed.

During the time of Jesus' persecution, all his disciples hid from him, and Peter even denied him three times. Something happened that caused all of them to have so much boldness and courage that they all died horrible deaths as martyrs except for John. When I learned about the resurrection and the historical evidence of what His disciples did and how they died, I began to believe. Jesus' own brother, James, doubted He was the Messiah until after the resurrection.

Today, I know that I know Jesus was and is "the way, the truth, and the life" (John 14:6) and not some insane, historical lunatic. Just like the disciples, you and I can decide to be and do anything. You just need to find the fuel. Doing the bare minimum will never be enough. That only leads to regret. The price is always paid. Whether it is the pain of discipline now or the pain of regret later is entirely up to you. I believe that an ounce of discipline is always worth more than a truckload of regret.

Hebrews 12:11 says, "No discipline seems pleasant at the time but painful. Later on, however, it produces a harvest of righteousness and peace for those who have been trained by it." Thinking and meditating on this verse has helped me trade in my perfectionist procrastinator philosophy for one that says,

> **An ounce of discipline is always worth**
> **more than a truckload of regret.**

"Don't put off until tomorrow that which you can accomplish today." *To have what you have never had you must do what you have never done. If you do what others won't, then you can have what others don't. It really is that simple!*

We all get to choose our time to be goal achieving or tension relieving. Doing what feels right in the moment isn't always the best decision.

5. Being disciplined is a key to happiness!

On a scale of one to ten with one being not so good and ten being incredible, where are you on the discipline scale? What is

anything was possible. My favorite definition of insanity is doing the same thing over and over and expecting a different result. New results require new perspective, activities, and choices.

Tens of thousands of people have turned their mess into a message of hope, freedom, and grace. Why shouldn't you? What's most important is how we react to life. No matter how hard we try, we will never control most of our circumstances. One of the only things we can truly control is our attitude. Just like we choose what shirt to wear, we get to choose what attitude to wear every day. It is definitely a fight and a process to learn to choose wisely. We can take action to improve our condition every single day. If there are things or people that contribute to negativity in your life, they must be removed or at a minimum limited. You are too blessed to be stressed. Here are the lyrics from my first original Christian song titled "I am free" to help to describe this concept.

It seems so long ago but then again I didn't know.

I was the one in control.

Living life so selfishly didn't care about anything.

I was losing my soul.

Take a walk with me.

To a place that I found recently.

Come take a walk with me.

It's time to let it go and fill our hearts with peace.

I am free. Free to believe.

I am free. Free to believe.

It's never easy to step out of the comfort zone when we're alone. I need you.

Always chasing something. Never stopping long enough to see the truth.

I walked in the darkness for far too long.

So full of fear and doubt, lost track of right and wrong.

I called to you, and you were waiting there for me.

To make it clear just where you wanted me to be.

I am free. Free to Believe.

I am free. Free to Believe.

You freed me from the pain.

You freed me from my fears.

You freed me from the chains.

Yeah you wiped away my tears.

You freed me from the pain.

You freed me from my fears.

You freed me from the chains.

Yeah you wiped away my tears.

I am free. Free to Believe.

I am free. Free to Believe.

It seems so long ago, but then again I didn't know.

I have never met the idiot who first said, "What you don't know won't hurt you," but I have learned what I did not know was ruining my life.

6. A key to *Finding Happy* is engaging in the battle and fighting for the things that are truly important.

What are the five most important things to you in your life right now, and how can you be more intentional in those areas?

_____

_____

_____

_____

_____

CHAPTER 12

AVA JAREE

I will never forget when my daughter Ava was born in 2008. I was still in the Army, stationed at Fort Bragg, and Ava was born in Fayetteville, North Carolina. It was the smoothest delivery because we actually had an appointment to be induced at the time, and at less than six pounds, Ava was much smaller than her older brother. Witnessing the miracle of her birth was fantastic. Even though I was already a father to a son, I knew that having a daughter was a game changer. This precious sweet princess was now part of our lives forever. I knew that I would do anything to take care of and protect her.

I will never forget driving home to grab a few things to take to the hospital and being completely overwhelmed from watching my daughter's birth. It was one of the best days of my life. I began to play a song I had co-written with my friend Wayne Tate, and I will never forget the happiness and joy that I felt in that moment.

Wayne was the worship leader at Manna Church at the time, and I had the opportunity to just sit in his office and create music during one of our meetings. Wayne and his wife, Rachel, are dear friends to this day and have been amazing examples for my wife and I. Wayne was a mentor to me for years, even meeting me on occasion for early breakfasts or driving all the way to our house to give and share his wisdom. He is an incredible human being.

Having a daughter was overwhelming at the time, but as I listened to the lyrics that God gave Wayne and I, I knew everything was going to be OK. Through my tears, all I could do was praise the creator of the universe and thank him once again for the incredible gift of life and blessing me with a baby girl. Here are some of the lyrics that were playing while I drove my car that day!

Lord, here I am to take a stand. Here I Am.

I give you all my days to follow you. Always.

When I am weak, you are my strength. You are all I need. I look and see your face. You rescued me. Amazing Grace.

Through Christ we overcome and the battle has been won. Through Christ we walk in victory. You're the same yesterday, tomorrow, and today. God of miracles, you're welcome in this place. Oh God of miracles, you're welcome in this place.

Today Ava is ten and loves all things horses. She is a total goofball and has the ability to light up a room the minute she enters. Her giggles keep us all laughing and smiling. She has stolen my heart forever.

I think of how we have God's heart and how he loves us so much that he sacrificed his only son Jesus Christ to give us a chance. He loves us far more than we could ever love any of our kids. He is Abba Father. Do you know him?

CHAPTER 13

BECOMING AN OFFICER

I couldn't shake the idea of becoming Colonel Kneller.

The seed that SFC Smith planted in me began to grow, and I found myself going through the process of becoming an officer. I applied with Southwestern College so I could complete my bachelor's degree. I spent most of my weekends from 2007 to 2009 studying and doing homework. After fifteen years and three times dropping out, I finally received a bachelor of arts with a focus in pastoral studies. Next, I had to make it through the officer board. You can imagine my surprise when I walked into the room and realized that I knew the woman running the board. She was a familiar face from church. It was confirmation for me that I was exactly where I was supposed to be.

After passing the board, I got my date to attend the officer candidate course at Fort Benning, Georgia. During this process we found out that we were going to have baby #3.

While Jaree was pregnant with Ava, she had a very interesting dream. She and I were arguing in her dream about what we would name the baby when God spoke and said, "He shall be named Elijah David." When she shared the dream, we were expecting a boy, and I agreed that Elijah would be a great name. Who am I to compete or argue with the Creator of the universe? You can imagine our surprise when we found out Elijah David was going to be a girl. Jaree began to believe that she had incorrectly interpreted the dream. After our daughter, Ava, was born, we didn't know whether we wanted to have any more children. We would talk about it once in a while, but were taking precautions to not have any accidental pregnancies. Sometime in early 2010, Jaree heard God speak to her and say, "Be fruitful and multiply." She told me what she had heard and so we stopped being cautious. When I found out a few days later that I might be deploying to Afghanistan, we resumed taking cautionary measures, but it was already too late. We were expecting.

> **God's timing is always perfect.**

Officer candidate school is a twelve-week course. Each day is filled with activities from sun up to sun down. I told Jaree that the only way I would be able to come home and see our new baby at the hospital would be if she had him on Veterans Day weekend. A tall order for sure, but you have to meet my wife. When she sets her mind to something, it is very rare that it does not happen the way she wants it to. Neither of us thought it would work out so perfectly, but she delivered our Elijah David on Veterans Day of 2010. I was amazed that my wife actually gave birth on the only weekend that I would be able to come home! I made it to the hospital just a few hours after he was born. I remember holding Elijah for the first time and once again being completely amazed. He is our God named Veterans Day baby. Today Gavin is thirteen, Ava is ten, and Elijah is seven, and they all bring me so much joy every single day. Having children is one of the most unexpected joys of my life.

CHAPTER 14

LEAVING FORT BRAGG

After completing officer training, it was time to head to Fort Sill, Oklahoma, to begin five months of field artillery officer training.

This meant packing up our life and moving on to the next duty station and new challenges. Jaree and I have such great memories of our time at Fort Bragg. It was a great time of learning, growing, and making lifelong friends. We were excited to be heading to a new place but also sad to say goodbye. As we were in the middle of this transition, a friend and I wrote a song to enter into a writing competition. We did not win, but the lyrics remind me of this season. It's called "Let's Just Drive."

And she tries to disguise all the tears in her eyes.

On the road as they go he just wants her to know.

That everything will be all right.

He sends a smile that says it all. It makes her cry.

And holds her hand really tight.

Starting over growing older got a real long drive.

He tells her everything will be all right.

Hold on for tomorrow. Let's just drive.

Memories make her smile and feel good inside.

Hold on for tomorrow. Let's just drive.

Baby, were gonna make it good tonight.

She turns up the radio and he wants to know.

How far can they take this car tonight?

She stares out through the window.

Five years later, and they finally got it right.

Doesn't matter what happened yesterday.

They value life in a whole new way.

Hold on for tomorrow. Let's just drive.

Memories make her smile and feel good inside.

Hold on for tomorrow. Let's just drive.

Baby, we're gonna make it good tonight.

Looking back to unwind at the life they left reflecting one
last time.

Looking back one last time they had to say goodbye.

To friends they left behind.

Looking back through the memories.

Holding on to all their dreams.

They used to want to get away.

Funny now how they want to stay.

Let's just drive, let's just drive, let's just drive oh baby let's just drive. Baby let's just drive.

Let's just drive, let's just drive, let's just drive oh baby let's just drive. Baby let's just drive.

Away.

Five months in Oklahoma and a month in Illinois, and we were off on our next adventure to Clarksville, Tennessee.

istan later that year. This meant that I would be gone for nine months.

The whole point of being a service member is to prepare for war and be ready to sacrifice whatever it takes to accomplish the mission. In 2012 three things happened that would drastically alter our family's future forever. These three things quickly opened my mind to a drastic and immediate career change. The first was learning of the death of Chase Prasnicki, the second was the surprise cancelation of my family vacation, and the third was not being available during a family crisis. At the beginning of 2012, I intended to serve in the military until I was forced to leave, and by the end of the year I couldn't leave fast enough.

I met Chase for the first time while going through field artillery officer training in 2011. He was a rare individual who was amazing in every way. It seemed as if everything he touched turned to gold. He was all-American in every sense of the word.

Chase was a West Point graduate and football alumni who could have done anything in life but chose to serve in the Army. Everyone who knew him loved him. He was a natural-born leader, incredible athlete, extremely intelligent, and he genuinely loved people. I cherish the time I had studying with him and our long conversations about leadership and marriage. After the officer course, twelve of us reported to ranger school and only Chase and one other made it straight through the school. Just another example of how gifted and talented this man was. Chase was married in November 2011, right before reporting to his first duty station in Germany. He was excited about his new adventure with family, career, and life.

In late June of 2012, I was in Fort Polk, Louisiana, training for an upcoming deployment when I got the tragic news. Chase had been deployed to Afghanistan, and on the fourth day he selflessly volunteered to lead a patrol. During the mission, his vehicle hit an IED, and he suffered catastrophic brain trauma. He passed away on June 27, 2012.

When I heard the news, it rocked me.

Chase was the last person that I thought this would happen to. He almost seemed invincible like some sort of super hero. Until this happened I had never even considered the idea that something bad could happen to me in the Army. This event reminded me of my own fragility. For the first time, I began to ask myself some of the hard questions. What if this happened to me? What would that look like for my family? Should I serve another ten years in the Army?

These questions led me to the realization that I wanted to do things that mattered with my family in a stable and safe environment.

Tomorrow is not promised to anyone.

Today is called the present because it is a gift.

Life is precious.

I wanted to leave a legacy that would be remembered by my grandchildren's grandchildren. Tomorrow is not promised to anyone. Today is called the present because it is a gift. Life is precious. First Lieutenant Chase Prasnicki was a true all-American who willingly laid down his life for his friends. He sacrificed himself so that our families could sleep in peace at night. I wear a memorial bracelet in honor of his sacrifice that reminds me to make each day count. Your days and mine are numbered, and we don't know how many we have left.

Reflecting on this story reminds me of Jesus Christ, who willingly laid down his life for the sins of the whole world. God loves you and me so much that he was willing to sacrifice his own son to give us all a chance. Today I am honored to shout

God's goodness from the rooftops and share about my friend, Lord and Savior King Jesus!

"For God so loved the world that he gave his one and only Son, that whoever believes in him shall not perish but have eternal life" (John 3:16).

The tragedy of life is not that it ends so soon, but that we wait so long to begin. Chase Prasnicki lived each day with intentionality and purpose. In his short twenty-four years, he lived so much life that hundreds packed into the church in Lexington, Virginia, for the funeral, and hundreds stood outside to listen through loudspeakers. His story is a constant reminder to me to make each day count and not just *exist* but *truly live!* His life is a reminder of selflessness. He served and gave so selflessly, and it's an example of how I want to be.

After I heard of his death, I viewed my upcoming deployment through a whole new perspective. This was not some video game where you get extra lives. This was a real enemy, with real bullets, in a country where most people did not like us nor want us there.

Should the unthinkable happen, I decided to take the family on an epic vacation before deploying. What better place to go to than Disney World? You can imagine my children's excitement when I shared the news that we would be heading to The Magical Kingdom of Disney in October 2012. My kids were counting down the days, and we had less then two weeks to go when I got the news. Some unexpected pre-deployment training came up, and I would have to cancel my vacation and save it for after.

The non-refundable Disney tickets didn't matter, and it was what it was. I could live with the vacation being canceled, but breaking the promise to my kids was almost too much to bear. I will never forget the streams of alligator tears rolling down my daughter's face when she said, "Daddy, you said we were going. Why can't we go?" Her little mind could not comprehend why I had to break my word to her. It was heartbreaking to cancel those plans with my kiddos. Due to my military commitment, I had to break trust with the ones who I cherished the most. At that moment I realized that I wasn't free at all and that the Army owned me.

The harsh reality was that as long as I was a soldier, I would not have time freedom, and my family would always get the leftovers. The military demands your best and your first. Although I thoroughly enjoyed training and leading soldiers for ten years, I wasn't sure I wanted to make sacrifices in this way for the next ten.

At the end of October, I deployed to Afghanistan and was stationed at Forward Operating Base (FOB) Joyce. My mission was to lead a small squad of six men and train the Afghan Army on how to operate their artillery. We would be responsible for three different locations and have to travel periodically to train, qualify, and oversee our Afghan artillery operations. While returning from training in Kabul we had a layover in the Bagram airport. This was one of the few places that had Wi-Fi access, so I jumped on the net to check on friends and family. My wife had recently made a post on Facebook about our son Elijah. Here is the post I read on December 21, 2012:

Elijah has Meckel's diverticulum. He is getting his blood transfusion now and is headed back for surgery. Please pray. This surgery is extremely risky because of the croup he was just diagnosed with on Tuesday. The doctor said the only reason they are doing the surgery now with all his breathing complications is because he's bleeding out faster than they can get blood in. Chances are he will have to be put on a ventilator for several days in order to keep him in stable respiratory condition. That means the machine will breathe for him while he's sedated. I'm a wreck and really need my spiritual family to cover us.

Love you all and will update soon.

When Elijah was just a few months old, we had noticed that he wasn't progressing like our other kids had. He didn't want to crawl or walk, so we began to have him tested. We found out that he was anemic, and the doctors labeled him failure to thrive and ended up telling us that he was iron deficient and possibly allergic to milk. I will never forget taking him to church one day and having a guest pastor pray over him. The pastor felt that God was leading him to tell us not to worry and that Elijah would grow up to be strong as an oak.

During this difficult time, I held on to those words "strong as an oak" that Michael Cotton had spoken over him. Once I read this, all I could think about was getting home. The only problem was that I was over 7,300 miles from home.

I immediately began to make arrangements to leave Afghanistan to go support my family. I assumed the plane ticket could be rerouted; I could sign my weapon over to my platoon sergeant and begin the journey home. But that wasn't the case. I had to fly the wrong direction, have a twenty-four-hour layover, and fly back to the airport all to sign a couple pieces of paper. I could not believe it. At that point, I mentally retired from the Army. I knew that I would have to make some serious changes before I could officially leave, but I realized as long as I was in the Army I would never have time freedom, and my family would always come second. I had a lot of time on the way home to do some thinking and began to formulate a plan to leave the Army.

I was able to arrive home on Christmas Eve of 2012, just hours after my son had been released from the hospital. I remember being so thankful to wake up on Christmas with us all back together.

CHAPTER 16

───── ⌁ ─────

GIVE UP THE GOOD
FOR THE GREAT

A few months before I deployed, one of Jaree's friends had reached out to her about a health product that she had gotten excited about. Jaree immediately began to investigate, and the more she learned, the more excited she became. She said she wanted to try the products, and if we liked them, then we could start our own business with the company.

I was excited about the idea but cautious. Just a few years before, we had gone through marital counseling concerning building side businesses and decided that I would focus on my Army career. I have always had an entrepreneurial spirit. In the fifth grade a friend and I started our own baseball card magazine. It was only eight pages long, but when we bought an ad to sell copies for a quarter we got a crazy response. Quarters started arriving in the mail every day.

The only problem is we hadn't calculated what postage would cost for us to send the magazine or the cost of paper and printer ink. So C and J Catalogs was a short-lived business venture. In my early twenties I would coordinate after-hours parties at the weigh station in which I lived. I would send out marketing teams to promote in the local bars and clubs. We would have people guiding cars in our parking lot, security in place, live entertainment, and all-you-could-drink beverages for $10 a person. Doing a couple of these a month paid the rent and all the utility bills. By my mid-twenties I was booking large venues and coordinating with radio stations to put on rock shows. I played around with a few other businesses over the years but could never seem to break through the $2000-a-month barrier with non-traditional work from home businesses.

We tried some of the health products with this new company and immediately fell in love with them. We jumped right in and started telling the world about what we had discovered. In our first month we earned over $2000, and in our second month we earned a $10,000 bonus that would be paid out to us $400 monthly for the next 25 months. The third month is when I deployed to Afghanistan.

When I came home for emergency leave to be with my family, it was originally only supposed to be for two weeks, but God had other plans. There was a vacancy at my unit, so I was asked to take over as the commander of my unit stateside. How fitting that my last position was a seat that I shouldn't have filled for at least another year but one that I aspired to lead from.

Because I was able to come home, we were able to attend a business conference in Jan of 2013. We were sitting in the audience, and our CEO put out this crazy promotion. He said, "If you can promote twice by March, you will earn a $25000 bonus." So Jaree looked at me and said, "Is that even possible?" I said, "Honey, through Christ all things are possible." I had heard that over and over, but I finally believed it. The truth of those words finally went from my head into my heart. During that weekend in Florida we saw all the people who had gone before us and already done what we were aspiring to do. We were so excited after that conference and went home super motivated to work and build something that could get me out of the military. We put our *why* into action and worked our butts off for 101 days.

We ended up being promoted three times and earned all kinds of bonuses, and I turned in a packet to get out of the Army. Before that, we had never been a six-figure family. Since that push, we've been a multiple six figure family ever since. We got so excited about this business that we earned over one million dollars in less then three years. For the last four years we have been top 100 earners with this company and have loved every minute of it.

> **When someone has a really strong *why***
> **and they put in the work, they will**
> **literally become unstoppable, and success**
> **becomes inevitable.**

I was recently honored to be on a leadership panel to share about the importance of a *why* on stage in front of about 20,000 people in Tampa, Florida.

When you have a strong *why* and are willing to put in the work, you become unstoppable, and your success becomes inevitable! The *why* is essential. Most people spend more time every year planning their two-week vacation than they do thinking about their life. Our *why* is what gives us the fuel to make serious changes. Our *why* is what makes our reasons strong and excuses very small. It's where our passion and our excitement come from. When someone has a really strong *why* and they put in the work, they will literally become unstoppable, and success becomes inevitable. That's how strong the *why* is.

interview a person who used to be depressed and is now happy. I once heard pastor Jim Frease of Joy Church say, "Don't be a know-it-all, be a learn-it-all."

Christian music artist Warren Barfield once played at a company event in Florida, and then I discovered that he only lives an hour from me. I bought his CD and the kids loved it, so I had the thought to track him down and invite him to lunch. After a few months of messaging back and forth with his assistant, two of my children and I met him for lunch, and it was wonderful. It was a lunch that my kiddos will never forget. They still bring it up years later. I don't think I have ever turned anyone down for lunch. Warren Buffet (my other favorite Warren) auctioned off a lunch, and the winner paid $650,000 just to have lunch with him. I have found that everyone loves to eat, so make some of your meals count.

Invite someone who has wisdom in an area you want to learn to a free lunch. John Maxwell, who has authored seventy-three books, buys someone lunch every month and has been doing so for over thirty years. He asks questions and takes notes. No wonder he is such a well of wisdom. Leaders are learners and leaders are readers. If you just read ten pages of a good book every day, that is a book a month. If you improve one-third of 1 percent per day, that equals over 100 percent a year. After five years you won't even recognize who you were five years ago. Seeking wisdom gives you hope. It shows that you can grow and you can change. To have more, you have to become more, and to become more, you have to grow in wisdom!

Are you a seeker of wisdom? What is the next book you plan on reading or the next class you plan on taking? Take action now!

_____

_____

_____

_____

_____

_____

 ## 7. Growing in wisdom is a key to happiness!

Become a Seeker of Truth

> *The truth is incontrovertible. Malice may attack it,*
> *ignorance may deride it, but in the end, there it is.*

Winston Churchill

There can only be one truth. If it's not the truth, then it is a lie. Satan is the father of lies and a thief. He wants to keep the truth from you and steal your joy. Sin often comes packaged in what appears to be happiness, but it is an illusion. Some sins may bring us temporary happiness, but in the end it's never worth the cost. Take a look at drug or alcohol addiction, fornication, or pornography. Each may bring temporary happiness, but at what cost? Sin keeps you longer than you want to stay and costs more than you want to pay, ultimately leaving you holding a bag full of shame and regret.

"The thief comes only to steal and kill and destroy; I have come that they may have life and have it to the full" (John 10:10).

To truly be happy, you have to know the truth. One of my favorite movies is *The Matrix,* and the dialogue between Neo and Morpheus does a great job explaining how I felt before I knew the truth.

Morpheus: I imagine that right now, you're feeling a bit like Alice. Hmm? Tumbling down the rabbit hole?

Neo: You could say that.

Morpheus: I see it in your eyes. You have the look of a man who accepts what he sees because he is expecting to wake up. Ironically, that's not far from the truth. Do you believe in fate, Neo?

Neo: No.

Morpheus: Why not?

Neo: Because I don't like the idea that I'm not in control of my life.

Morpheus: I know exactly what you mean. Let me tell you why you're here. You're here because you know something. What you know you can't explain, but you feel it. You've felt it your entire life, that there's something wrong with the world. You don't know what it is, but it's there, like a splinter in your mind, driving you mad. It is this feeling that has brought you to me. Do you know what I'm talking about?

This is exactly how I felt before I began to discover the truth. I knew that I was made for more, but I didn't know what I was supposed to do, and I wasn't ready for it at the time. The truth is that God loves you, he wants what's best for you, and you can trust him. If you feel the way that Neo felt or the way that I felt, then know that all the answers are available.

The truth rarely just comes to you.
You have to go out and get it. It's a
treasure that is available to all but only
a few ever discover.

Jesus answered, "I am the way and the truth and the life. No one comes to the Father except through me" (John 14:6).

To the Jews who had believed him, Jesus said, "If you hold to my teaching, you are really my disciples. Then you will know the truth, and the truth will set you free" (John 8:31–32).

My first attempt at writing a Christian rock song was entitled "TRUTH" and embodies these principles. Here are some of the lyrics.

Don't wait another second.

Put your trust in HIM.

You can believe you are set free.

Don't you know that you're truly alive.

That's why he came and died.

And by the way his cup it satisfies, yeah.

Seek the truth and,

It will set you free.

Don't close your eyes, don't blind your mind,

Because you'll never see.

In my weakness I grow stronger, Paul would say. With your help, Lord, we can do this.

Show me the way.

Seek the truth and,

It will set you free.

Don't close your eyes, don't blind your mind,

Because you'll never see.

8. When you know the truth, you begin to know your creator. This is a key to *Finding Happy!*

Along the way to learning the truth, we must always tell the truth.

People who tell the truth don't have to remember what they said before. I was a sneaky teenager who often lied to my parents. On the occasions that I did get caught, my father would ask why I did all these silly things when I knew I would get caught. I would just shrug my shoulders and give my stock answer to most questions, which was, "I don't know." He would go on to tell me that I would always get caught. The reality was my parents maybe caught me once out of every ten to fifteen times

> **Be more concerned with your character than your reputation, because your character is what you really are, while your reputation is merely what others think you are.**

I did something wrong. This became very dangerous in my life because the odds were drastically in my favor for getting away with it. What I realize now is that each lie, manipulation, and hurt was sowing the seeds of disaster. I have learned that time will always promote or expose you.

I have been exposed over the years by being demoted, ticketed, divorced, bankrupt, sick, depressed, sad, and almost homeless. Over the last ten years, I have begun to be promoted and become influential. I've worked hard and been promoted in unexplainable ways. Debts have mysteriously fallen off my credit report, opportunities have fallen into my lap, I've become close friends with the most incredible people, my children are amazing, my father has become the dad I had always hoped for, my business has prospered, and marriage has gotten to a level I never thought possible.

John Wooden said it best when he wrote, "Be more concerned with your character than your reputation, because your character is what you really are, while your reputation is merely what others think you are."

Always tell the truth because if you don't have your character and integrity, then you have nothing!

CHAPTER 18

YOU WERE MADE
FOR MORE

I love numbers, and I always love the underdog.

The odds are stacked against us to accomplish anything great in this life. Statistically, you and I are supposed to get divorced, have massive debt, be miserable, and have children who cause us pain and heartache. So, what is different about that minority of marriages that last? The ones who live debt free, the couples who view Mondays the same as Fridays, and the families who have kids that save their first kiss for their honeymoon? How can you and I hope to live a life that we know most will not? A life like the one just described? Here is the key. Do what most others will never do so that you can have what most others will never have. Do not surrender your future or settle for the crumbs of life just to fit in with the flock to appear normal.

What is normal anyway? I once heard it explained like this, "Normal is getting dressed in clothes that you buy for work and driving through traffic in a car that you are still paying for in order to get to the job you need to pay for the clothes and the car, and the house you leave vacant all day so you can afford to live in it." If that's normal, then I don't want any part of it. My advice is that when everyone else is going with the flow and drifting downstream, you should swim upstream. If everyone else is running east, then you go west. When everyone else is watching television, you read books. When everyone else is checking out after his or her eight-hour workday, you can build a part-time business or develop a talent. Take control of your future, and decide what it is that you want. Spend some time every day designing your ideal life. That is how you push. That is how you succeed. Break the monotonous cycle, and make moves that place you closer to your goals. If you do not make time for your goals, then you spend time working for someone else who did.

I once heard a very wise man say that if it's been a long time since you've done something for the first time, then it's about time.

What is something that you can start today that will help you beat the odds?

---

 9. Being productive and beating the odds is a key to happiness.

Years ago, I had the pleasure of attending the Restoration House Church in Hopkinsville, Kentucky, for a season and learning from Pastor Brad Fancher. The culture at this church is all about loving on people. It was an incredible environment.

Pastor Brad went through a series called Made for More. I was so inspired by it that I started a company called Made for More, Inc. and have been doing annual "men's retreats" ever since. The most incredible things have happened there. This year we had one guy who wanted to get baptized. As my friend Delane and I went to go baptize him, another guy felt led to get baptized. After these two, another guy came into the water, then another, and then another. That night another guy decided he wanted to get baptized, and the following morning four more guys went into the water. A total of nine men decided to get baptized at an event with around 110 men.

These guys were wrecked at this retreat. It was incredible to witness it. This retreat was in September 2017, and it is still impacting lives today. A gentleman who traveled to the US for the first time from the UK to attend the retreat went home and got baptized. Changing lives is the best feeling in this world. If you're reading this now and you're not connected to another man, or you're married and not connected to another couple, get connected. Each one of us needs someone in the trenches fighting for our lives, our marriages, and our kids. We need like-minded warriors who stand beside us.

All of us need each of us, and each of us need all of us.

Jim Rohn

Who are five people who you are making an intentional effort to connect with?

_____

_____

_____

_____

_____

Every year as the holidays come around, we have our tradi-
tions of getting together with friends and family. I didn't really
understand the importance of this while I was a child, but I have
so many wonderful memories to look back on now. We would
go to my grandma's house every single year for certain holidays
and then rotate through the family to attend other dinners and
events at different family members' homes. I don't remember
there really being any drama, just family enjoying each other's
company. It was a good time for all in attendance.

We were created in the image of God, and we know that God
values relationships. What baby doesn't like the cuddling of its
mother or father? As we get older, we sometimes isolate and
alienate ourselves from relationships, which isn't what we were
created to do. We often try and get people to pay us the debts

> **Betrayal is what someone does to you, and
> bitterness is what you do to yourself.**

that someone from our past may owe. If you were betrayed, let
down, or lied to in the past, that doesn't mean the next person in
your life will do the same, and they don't owe you from someone else's faults and limitations. The enemy wants you bitter,
not better. Don't allow what has happened to you or what was
done to you define you. Betrayal is what someone does to you,
and bitterness is what you do to yourself. Proverbs 17:22 says,
"A cheerful heart is good medicine, but a crushed spirit dries up
the bones."

I was so skeptical of people for the longest time. I vowed to
never be burned again. I had many years of trust issues, and I was
lonely for a very long time. Sometimes we allow the enemy to
lie to us and take us deeper down a path of darkness.

What paths have you unwittingly walked that God never intended for you? Now is the time to evaluate it and maybe let some things go.

I've learned to forgive quickly but trust slowly and in increments. Even the Lone Ranger has his friend Tonto. We all need special people with whom we can explore life. We were created to develop relationships with people. This was God's plan from the start. It seems that God himself desires relationships. He didn't have to create the angels or any of us. Everything that we believe and know to have value started as a seed that was planted in us by another person. The important part is to know who has your ear. Your motivation comes from your associations. I believe that every person should have at least five people in their inner circle. I call it the circle of five. These are the people with whom you can be vulnerable and share your darkness. These are the people who are for you, your marriage, and your success. They know everything about you and like you anyway. They come with no strings attached. They are mature enough to not be jealous of you or add to your self-limiting beliefs. They are your biggest cheerleaders, and you are theirs. You are the sum of the five people whom you hang around with the most. Be aware of who is influencing you. If you spend most of your time hanging around a bunch of bums, then before long you may start acting like a bum. In order to grow and progress forward, we must spend time with people who challenge us to be the best version of ourselves.

My friend Pastor Jim Frease from Joy Church says, "Some relationships need to be initiated, some cultivated, and some terminated." I completely agree! Take a moment today to think about what or whom you need to let go.

CHAPTER 19

DETERMINE HOW YOU WANT TO BE REMEMBERED NOW

The way you live your life is in your hands.

One of my favorite books of all time is *The Seven Habits of Highly Effective People* by Steven Covey. One of the seven habits is to begin with the end in mind.

The point of this habit is to approach your life like you would approach building a home. It wouldn't be smart to start building a house until it is already done on paper. We call this the blueprint. You have to have a vision for your life. The Bible says in Proverbs 29:18, "Where there is no vision the people perish." That was all I needed to know. We cannot be like a hobo or a drifter and expect to fulfill our purpose. By default, failure to plan is planning to fail.

Habakkuk 2:2 says: "And the LORD answered me, and said, write the vision, and make it plain upon tablets, that he may run that reads it." It's not good enough to just have goals. You have to write them down and become accountable to someone to accomplish them. They also need to be yours, be specific, and have a deadline for their attainment.

Remember that '80s rock song "Here I Go Again" by Whitesnake? The lyrics help make this point.

I don't know where I'm going,

But I sure know where I've been.

Hanging on the promises,

In songs of yesterday.

An' I've made up my mind,

I ain't wasting no more time,

But, here I go again.

Here I go again.

Tho' I keep searching for an answer,

I never seem to find what I'm looking for.

Oh Lord, I pray.

You give me strength to carry on,

'Cause I know what it means.

To walk along the lonely street of dreams.

An' here I go again on my own.

Goin' down the only road I've ever known,

Like a hobo I was born to walk alone.

An' I've made up my mind.

I ain't wasting no more time.

I'm just another heart in need of rescue,

Waiting on love's sweet charity.

An' I'm gonna hold on.

For the rest of my days,

'Cause I know what it means.

To walk along the lonely street of dreams.

Here I go again on my own.

Going down the only road I've ever known.

Like a drifter, I was born to walk alone,

And I've made up my mind.

I ain't wasting no more time. Here I go again.

This is how most people live life: drifting, waiting, and hoping.
You don't have to walk alone. The God of the universe desires
to have a personal relationship with you. The Bible says that if
you draw close to him, then he will draw close to you. He won't
force you though. My favorite definition of insanity is doing the
same thing over and over and expecting a different result. Rarely
will a good idea interrupt you. Two of the best days of your life
will be the day you were born and the day you figure out *why*
you were born. It will take some time, but when you begin to
figure that out, then you will know which direction to travel.
What is your life mission statement? Have you ever thought
about it? I didn't until I was almost forty years old. No wonder I
was randomly drifting for so many years. I had no vision for my
life. I hadn't tried to discover why I was born.

One day I read this vision statement of Paul J. Meyer, who adopted his vision statement from John Wesley, and I just knew it was the very reason I was created.

It says:

"Do all the good you can

By all the means you can

In all the ways you can

In all the places you can

At all the times you can

To all the people you can

As long as ever you can."

Remember that in late 1999 and early 2000s, I was at the lowest point in my life. I was a musician who was actually sabotaging my life with the very songs I was writing. Proverbs 18:21 says that there is the power of life and death in the tongue. Every time I sang the very lyrics of songs I had written, I was speaking death over my own life. What words are you choosing to speak over your life and others?

One song I wrote was titled "Torture Train," and it was a self-fulfilling prophecy every time I sang the lyrics.

The games you play. I often want to break your neck. I told you, I promised I would never change. And that's exactly why I'm still the same.

Your happiness and mine was always a shade away. Next thing I know I've been taken by the rage. I told you never to set foot on the Torture train. You didn't listen and so now you've gone insane.

> The Torture train will break you. An event that leads into
> self-destruction is what we're addressing here. The train
> will force you. It will force you to go insane. Go insane
> and change the way you think. Don't think.

No wonder I was in such a dark place here. I was angry, full of
rage, and constantly telling myself to not change and not think.
It doesn't get much worse than that. This is a huge reason why I
was so miserable for so long. Maybe you have been there or are
there right now. Always remember that happiness is an inside job,
and it is something that you have to *believe* is possible to have on
a consistent basis before you actually *feel* those emotions consistently. The ball is in your court. If you are willing to change, then
everything will change for you!

My parents recently spent about a year living with us. They
had just retired, and we had the extra space in our house. We all
thought it would be a great chance for our kids to get to know
their grandparents on a deeper level. The Army had kept us from
our family for the greater part of the last decade, so we thought
it would be fun to have them live with us. We originally expected this to last for three to six months, but they ended up staying
about a year. You may be thinking that would be a horrible idea
to have your family or in-laws stay with you, but it was better
for us than we could have imagined. The most memorable part
of that year was waking up to this strange noise that my father
would make.

My father can be very loud, so you could imagine my surprise
when I would wake up from a dead sleep to hear him singing
in the most out-of-tune voice you can imagine. I wish the Bible
had been more specific to only make a joyful noise if it is in
tune, but it doesn't clarify. Many mornings I would wake up to
this song.

> This is the day, this is the day that the Lord has made, that
> the Lord has made.

I will rejoice, I will rejoice and be glad it is, and be glad it is.

This is the day that the Lord has made; I will rejoice and be glad it is.

This is the day; this is the day that the Lord has made.

I have to admit, the first few times I heard this, I would become extremely irritated and shove a pillow over my head and pray it would stop. After a few times of this occurring, something crazy happened. I began to hear the kids joining in. A few times Jaree and I were even awake early enough to join in too. My parents don't live with us anymore (they moved on to Florida life), but recently we had other family stay with us who had heard the story and asked if we would sing it with them also. A new tradition is born, and I got to see it unfold. I will never forget seeing my children jump up and down smiling, singing, and dancing with their grandma and grandpa. My kids will never forget the smile my father has every single morning when he sings that song or the loving heart of my mother. He will tell you that each day he gets to make a choice and today is a great day to choose joy.

Make intentional good choices with your thoughts and words, and always remember that the power of life and death is in the tongue.

CHAPTER 20

JUST DO IT

Whatever you vividly imagine, ardently desire, sincerely believe, and enthusiastically act upon must inevitably come to pass.

Paul J. Meyer

When it comes to most things in life, I have learned that if someone can do it, then most people can do it. Now, I'm not talking about slam-dunking a basketball, winning American Idol, or memorizing a fifty-page book in fifteen minutes. A few people can do those things, but most cannot, no matter how hard they try.

I'm talking about the things that anyone can do but most don't. I'm talking about being a good parent or spouse, losing twenty pounds, or saving $10,000. These are all things that are possible for anyone and everyone. So if they are possible, then why don't most people do them? I'm glad you asked. It's because most people are apathetic and focused on their circumstances changing instead of them changing. "If only my job would pay more," says the poor man as he sinks into his chair to binge-watch Netflix for the fifth year in a row.

In life we have the things we must do and then extra time to spend on tension relieving or goal achieving. Most people spend 95 percent of their free time on tension relieving. We live in a microwave society where people want it fast, and they want it now. The truth is that's not how God created you to be. God didn't create you to live in survival mode twenty-four hours a day. He created you for joy. Be patient on the journey, and realize that your timing isn't His.

Most things that are truly worthwhile in life take time. Just as Rome was not built in a day, neither will our lives be. We have to build our lives day by day and brick by brick.

I've learned to continuously ask myself, "What are you building?" Challenge yourself to build more and know why you are building it. What are you intentionally building each day?

_____

_____

_____

_____

_____

Have You Ever Gone All In?

I have been to a few casinos over the years and lost money every time. The odds are stacked in the dealer's favor, and the system preys on the pride and greed of every person who is willing to gamble. The casino is barely a step up from playing the lottery. However, there is one game that I really enjoy the concept behind, Texas Hold'em. I have never played it at a casino, but I love the challenge and competition of it. We play sometimes at our house when the in-laws are visiting or with friends. It's people playing against people. Not the house taking in the dough from you and I. There is something very special about it and something that I believe is essential to *Finding Happy*. There comes a time in the game when you decide to go "all in." You push all your chips into the middle of the table and go for it. You are going to have one of two possible outcomes: one, you are either going to lose everything and be out of the game, or two, you are going to win *big*!

I *love* winning *big*; do you? Whether it's Texas Hold'em or life, when you go all in, you are positioning yourself to have a massive breakthrough. When you win in the game, your confidence is increased. When you win in life, you discover why you were created. I haven't won every time I have gone all in with Texas Hold'em, but I have every time I've gone all in in life.

> **Commitment is doing what you said you would do long after the feeling you said it in has left you.**

When you take this position with your life, it's like fate, time, and circumstances have a meeting, and they say he or she is going to do it or die, so you might as well let him or her have it. I'm not talking about going all in from a position of fear or desperation, I'm talking about effort, commitment, resolve, and Holy Spirit stubbornness. Commitment is doing what you said you would do long after the feeling you said it in has left you. Resolve is saying I will keep going until I get to where I want to be. When was the last time you went all in? *When you find something worth going all in for, you will gladly stay up late and wake up early, and you will be on track to* Finding Happy!

Your Past Does Not Have to Equal Your Future.

Sometimes you have to get to the root of the challenges in your life by doing a checkup from the neck up.

Has it ever occurred to you that things that happened years or decades ago are affecting you today? Years ago I learned about a ministry called RTF (Restoring the Foundations). Jaree and I went through a full week multiple times with this ministry, and it was life changing. We discovered many things that were holding us back from all God intended us to be. We discovered ungodly beliefs that were blocking us from walking out our calling and destiny. We discovered roots where the enemy planted seeds that grew into skepticism, doubt, fear, and pessimism. So many of us are prisoners of our past. We feel unworthy because of the lies that we have come into agreement with. Knowledge is power; what you don't know today is hurting you. You have to get to the root of why you are the person you are today and how you can position yourself to grow and change.

I had a memory during one of the ministry sessions of an event that happened when I was a small child. My parents and I went to the beach, and my father swam way out into the ocean. My mom was scared and upset about that, and it planted a seed of distrust in me. The enemy warped the event and made me believe that my dad didn't care about me and was willing to risk his life in the ocean. This voice said, "Be careful because your father is careless and reckless. Don't trust him." I began to view many things through that skewed lens throughout my life. I remember thinking I had to be adopted and looking for evidence throughout the house. I felt abandoned. I was lending my ear to the wrong voice. It is key to understand what voice has your attention.

When you understand the root of the problem, you are on your way to healing. When you gain this wisdom, you are on your way to *Finding Happy*.

Leave a Legacy

You have a choice to make today. Will your grandchildren's children know you? You don't have to meet them or be alive for this to happen. They can know you by the stories and the impact that you created. If you add value to your children and grandchildren's lives, then of course they will be impacted. The major motivation behind this book is to share with you, my children, grandchildren, and many future generations. The idea that something I say here may affect my children's great-grandchildren is very exciting for me. I want to be remembered. I want thousands of lives to be better because of my life. You can want and accomplish the same thing.

I remember reading and thinking about all I could share but not having a clue how to do it. I challenge you to live a life worth sharing with your grandchildren's grandchildren. It will bring you so much happiness to know that you are leaving a legacy that can continue for hundreds or thousands of years!

Sometimes we get in our own way. We overthink, overanalyze, and remain stuck. Don't stay stuck.

Just Show Up

One of the best pieces of advice I could ever give anyone is to just show up. Show up for the marriage conference, go to the game, visit the church, watch the webinar, and go to the wedding. I've often heard that to go up you have to show up. It takes about 10,000 hours to become an expert at anything, and it's going to take some time and intention to become a consistently happy and joyful person. When you find someone who is walking in true happiness, get around him or her as often as you can. Ask them how they became the way they are. You have to go out and ask the questions and find the answers. Rarely will a good idea interrupt you, and the book you do not read cannot help you.

I meet people all the time who have never flown, visited another state, or ventured out of their comfort zone in any way, shape, or form. This often leads to a very lonely and isolated life. Always remember that loneliness or happiness are both choices that you get to make. There are people meeting every day in your city to talk about all kinds of things. Consider joining a small group at church, downloading the Meetup app on your phone, or joining some kind of city event. There are incredible people meeting all around you, and if you don't join or you don't go you will never know what could have been.

What I do know is that you are missing out.

If Jaree and I had never attended our first church or sought out mentors, we wouldn't have discovered all the extraordinary things that have led us to where we are now. If I wouldn't have attended my friends' wedding, I wouldn't have met Steve Crowther, which means no destiny and calling class or mission trips to Brazil.

If we hadn't found Manna Church in 2005, then we wouldn't have many of the incredible relationships that we have today. If we hadn't joined the worship team, then we wouldn't have developed the relationships with the Tate's or Rebecca Graham, who was our RTF minister. If I didn't say yes to meeting my sister on her birthday, then I never would have met Josh Denne. If I hadn't gone to the event in Ohio with Josh, then I never would have been introduced to the world of personal development.

If I wouldn't have joined the band and agreed to play at the benefit, I might have never met the love of my life. Every choice leads to the next choice, and it all requires *action*! Routines are great, but sometimes you have to break the norm to step into the new. Embrace the seasons of change in your life, and instead of being anxious, nervous, or scared about the next move or change, get excited about it!

What changes do you feel like you need to make but haven't made yet?

_____

_____

_____

_____

CHAPTER 21

HAPPINESS IS A
DECISION

I have learned that happiness will never be a constant because life happens. Feeling pleasure, enjoyment, or glad because of life circumstances is amazing but usually short-lived. We can't gauge our life by our feelings. Many people chase the things they think they want, only to find out it wasn't really what they wanted in the first place. The nights I played shows with the rock bands were incredible, but the loneliness afterwards was unbearable. Isn't it ironic that what God created for good, in musical gifts, could be counterfeited and used for evil?

I think that's a reason why so many musicians commit suicide. They aren't ready for the fame and fortune, and the pressure crushes them. They often turn to medication and drugs. When the fame fades away, they get tired of mentally reliving how great they remember the past being. They miss the feeling of being important. Some people never discover that their feeling of importance shouldn't come from man! We also see this occur in athletes and actors. They look back to the glory days and live life as if the best days are behind them. What if I told you that your best days were ahead of you?

I remember thinking I only had until I was twenty-seven years old to live; now, as each year goes by, I enjoy it more and more. Today is a gift, which is why it is called the "present."

Finding Happy starts with a decision. It's deciding that you are going to be happy and starting off each day with an attitude of gratitude. In the Army we called it hunting the good stuff. We all have so much to be thankful for. I wake up thankful for where I live, to have running water, three healthy children and an amazing wife, a successful business, friends that know all about me and like me anyway, and pets that bring my children and wife happiness.

Sometimes I'm just happy because the people I love are happy. The key is deciding to be happy. The word "decide" is powerful. Homicide means causing the death of someone else, suicide means causing the death of your own self, and "decide" means the death to all other options. As humans we can make any decision we want any time we want. *The Christmas Carol* movie is a great example of this. Ebenezer Scrooge is a massively wealthy, miserable man, and he decides to make his life count. By the end of the movie we see how he ultimately receives so much more by how he gives to others. *You can't take with you what you got, but you can take with you what you give.*

Hold On for Just Another Day

So many people are breathing but not living.

There is definitely purpose beyond your pain. I went through days where I could barely breathe after my younger brother died and relationships failed. I would just hang on to the possibility that tomorrow could be a little better. Each day brings new hope and opportunity. I was going through some boxes the other day and found a CD I had recorded many years ago, and I had completely forgotten about. One song is titled "Let It Go." Mine was written long before the movie *Frozen* came out. The chorus goes:

> Hold on for just another day.
>
> Stay strong, everything's gonna be OK.
>
> Moving on, good things are gonna come your way.
>
> Let it go.
>
> Let your troubles fade away.

Decide today to become an eternal optimist instead of a broken pessimist. No matter how bad things might get or seem, always remember that you are one night's sleep away from a new perspective. Never, ever lose hope!

What are you thankful for right now, and what are you hopeful for?

_____

_____

_____

_____

_____

 # 10. Always getting your hopes up is a key to finding happiness.

Give Your Happiness an Upgrade

I believe that anyone can be happy but only someone who knows Jesus can have true joy. Joy is a *great* feeling of pleasure and happiness. It's like happiness on steroids. When I was not a Christian, I would often mistake joy as some foreign, fake feeling that served no purpose!

I always looked forward to our family events each year while growing up. I always felt extremely awkward though around one relative, my Aunt Pat.

Aunt Pat is my mom's brother's wife and one of the sweetest people on the planet. I don't have a single memory of my Aunt Pat not being extremely joyful. She was always smiling and genuinely happy to see everyone. All those years growing up, I questioned her authenticity because I couldn't understand how anyone could be as excited and happy about life as she was. I had no reference for that type of joy, and so it didn't seem real. She would tell you it is all about her faith and relationship with her Lord and Savior Jesus Christ. After I gave my life to Jesus, I began to experience that same joy and supernatural peace that surpasses all understanding. It is the best feeling in the world that I hope you can experience also.

> *Do not be anxious about anything, but in every situation by prayer and petition, with thanksgiving, present your requests to God. And the peace of God, which transcends all understanding, will guard your hearts and your minds in Christ Jesus.*

Phil. 4:6-7

My Aunt Pat is a living, breathing example of what the peace of God looks like.

CHAPTER 22

MAKE EACH DAY YOUR MASTERPIECE

I remember in middle school having a numbers-writing contest with my buddy Jeff. We just wanted to see who could write more numbers, so we filled out pages and pages and pages of numbers. I think I stopped somewhere around 40,000. Did you know that there are 1,440 minutes in a day and 86,400 seconds? There are 43,200 minutes in a typical month and 525,600 minutes in the year. In the Army you are taught to accomplish things in ten-minute increments. There is no hour getting ready for something, there is ten minutes. You often get ten-minute bathroom breaks, ten minutes to eat, ten minutes to make a phone call, etc. In our business we schedule twenty-minute personal calls and sixty-minute team meetings. I schedule time with my family. When you are self-employed, the calendar becomes your boss. The great thing is that you are in charge of your calendar.

The bottom line is the clock is ticking, and we don't get the time back that we waste. I promise you that no one currently residing in a nursing home would tell you that they regret not wasting more time. They would tell you they should have spent more time doing things that mattered with people who cared. They wish they would have taken more risks, apologized more, smiled more, and loved more.

The older I get, the faster the time goes by. I think much differently in my forties than I did in my twenties. Don't be the person who dies old and lonely choking on the dust of your own regret.

CHAPTER 23

ALAN WINTER: THE GENERAL OF UNITY

When I went on my first missions trip to Brazil, I got to meet an incredible guy named Alan Winters. He was the closest to a real-life Indiana Jones I have ever met. Alan and his wife, Heidi, founded Frontline Missions. This is a ministry that goes and serves the hidden and forgotten people of the world in Colombia, Venezuela, Brazil, Honduras, and many other places.

The Winters have dedicated their lives to being the hands and feet of Jesus. Alan suffered a stroke on his way to Cartagena, Colombia, in early 2017. After many roadblocks, the family was finally able to medevac him back to the States, where he had several surgeries and passed away on March 1, 2017. I attended his funeral on Wednesday March 15, 2017, and it was unlike anything I had ever experienced.

It was a celebration of life. Even though it was a Wednesday afternoon, there were thousands in attendance. I learned that Alan had gone on over 400 mission trips with thousands of people. More then half in attendance at the funeral had gone on a trip with Alan. Alan's son said that his father ran his race so well that he got to go to heaven first. At the end of the funeral, the family lined up at the front of the church facing the audience and led everyone in a worship song. Instead of the crowd comforting the family, the family actually began to comfort the crowd. It was the most incredible thing I had ever seen. The Winters have dedicated their lives to service, and service to many leads to greatness.

That funeral changed my life in a profound way.

Alan was called the general of unity because he had a special way of bringing everyone together in Atlanta, Georgia, and all over the world. He was known to bring people from all different backgrounds and denominations with him on his trips. He simply loved people. He was the most unselfish individual I have ever met. God wants to be known, and he used Alan in a mighty way. What is so amazing is that the same DNA that Alan had is in you and I.

Alan was a great testimony to God's love. Alan shared the heart of God in his love and grace. He came to everyone as a friend and not with a big stick to discipline. You and I need to be able to reach the hearts of the broken. We need to hear their stories and let the Holy Spirit use us to heal them. Trust has to be built. It's important to take off the hat of truth and discipline and demonstrate His love to as many people as we can. It's his kindness that draws us to repentance.

We have to learn to partake of God's goodness so that we can share with others how good he is so they can experience it in their own way. Teach people to be givers. Not out of the law but out of the gratefulness of God. Giving might look many different ways. We can learn a lot from the people who go before us. Who can you watch on YouTube? Which pastors and leaders can you read about and learn from? There's plenty of wisdom and knowledge out there. Learn from legends. Make it your goal to learn from legends.

Alan Winters was a man of peace in every area. He was a man of love toward all of those who were missed by others. He was a man of unity. He could look into people's hearts and see who they could be and would be, and he helped them get there. Alan lived more in his fifty-eight years than most do in a hundred.

Do you have any people in your life like my Aunt Pat or Alan Winters? I challenge you to get around them more. Who are three people who you can be intentional about getting around more and learning from?

_____

_____

_____

_____

_____

A CALL TO ACTION

I challenge you to live a life worthy of your calling and destiny. Start where you are now, and grow a little each day. No matter where you are on your journey or how much farther you think you have to go, get out of your own way. Stop overthinking and overanalyzing every step. Have faith and move because God blesses effort.

Live an intentional life.

Live a life full of passion, excitement, courage, happiness, and joy.

Do things that matter with people who care. Take risks, be a difference maker, experience different cultures, and share God's love with as many people as you can. Study the Bible, become a disciple, and then practice what you have learned and teach it to others.

Your life is not a dress rehearsal, so make it count.

Make each day your masterpiece, hunt the good stuff, and have an attitude of gratitude. Serve as many people as you can as often as you can and pay the price of discipline today instead of the price of regret later. Be strong, live well, and enjoy the journey!

**Now the Lord is the Spirit, and where the
Spirit of the Lord is, there is freedom.**

2 Cor. 3:17

Dear reader,

I know that this is a lot to chew on. You may be hearing some of these ideas for the first time, or maybe you have heard them before and dismissed or forgotten them.

What are you chasing? Every day, we are all chasing something whether it's subconscious or intentional. Some chase money, some chase relationships, and some chase fame. Maybe you are chasing fulfillment or recognition because you have never felt special, fulfilled, or recognized. I challenge and urge you to chase God and his son Jesus. All the answers are in the pursuit of loving the Lord your God with all your heart, all your soul, and your entire mind. Learn to not chase empty things that will only leave you lonely and tired.

So many people chase things to only find out years later that it wasn't what they really wanted. It's empty and shallow happiness that is usually wrapped in sin. Become a person who is known for your faith. You will have to become aware of your fears and push them into a small corner. Anyone can see a problem, but it takes courage to solve it. Since the beginning of time there has been a battle between darkness and light. It seems that without one, there wouldn't be the other. We need fear to understand faith, and we need darkness to understand light.

Because of this, embrace the struggle; it will greatly improve your future reward. If I were to go to the local college, grab a football, and sprint from the fifty-yard line to the end zone, would we call it a touchdown? I think not. It's only a touchdown when you dodge and evade the 300-pound pass rushers and break through the secondary who all are trying to smash you! So the struggle is necessary, and it is a process. I've heard that failure is the fertilizer of success, so embrace it. Nothing great happens without a struggle.

As you go through this process of growth and change, you will face many tests. When you see yourself running into the same mountain over and over, just know that God is patient and kind. He will let you retake the test as many times as it takes. He will also not give you more than you can handle. Let your situations and circumstances cause you to run to him. After you pass each test, there will always be more training and more tests forever, so embrace the process.

If any of these ideas have helped, I would love to hear from you, so please send an email to findinghappy1@yahoo.com, and make sure and go to www.everymanawarrior.com for other books to assist you in walking out your calling and destiny.

Until All Have Heard,
Chad Kneller
#MADEFORMORE
#FINDINGHAPPY

ABOUT THE AUTHOR

Chad Kneller is the founder and CEO of Made For More Inc., a company dedicated to bridge the gap between reality and possibilities for aspiring entrepreneurs. Mr. Kneller served as an Army officer after pursuing a music career in the rock and roll industry. He represented the US Army in 2009 in Operation Rising Star and was a top six international finalist. He's had the opportunity to speak in front of tens of thousands of entrepreneurs over the last six years and is a highly sought-after sales trainer in the field of health and wellness. Chad and his wife, Jaree, have a strong passion to coach married couples to not only survive but thrive. Mr. Kneller has three children: Gavin is thirteen, Ava is ten, and Elijah is seven. They reside in Tennessee.

MEET CHAD KNELLER
FOLLOW HIM

FACEBOOK & TWITTER@
CHAD KNELLER

EMAIL @
MADEFORMOREINC@GMAIL.COM

WEBSITE @
WWW.FINDINGHAPPYBOOK.COM

WWW.MADE4MORE.BIZ

DONATE TO HIS FAVORITE CHARITY AT
WWW.THEDARKLOSES.COM

CONNECT WITH A MENS GROUP AT
WWW.EVERYMANAWARRIOR.COM